AMERICA THE GREATEST, BUT...

Harold W. Powell

authorHOUSE®

AuthorHouse™
1663 Liberty Drive, Suite 200
Bloomington, IN 47403
www.authorhouse.com
Phone: 1-800-839-8640

First published by AuthorHouse 9/22/2008

ISBN: 978-1-4343-9333-3 (sc)
ISBN: 978-1-4343-9334-0 (hc)

Printed in the United States of America
Bloomington, Indiana

This book is printed on acid-free paper.

Book Cover Photo Courtesy of Sue Collins

1. INTRODUCTION   1

2.AMERICA THE GREATEST BUT-----   5

3. ECONOMY INDEPENDENCE OR BANKRUPTCY   18

4.THE SHOCKING TRUTH ABOUT THE ELECTRIC
UTILITIES AND THE POTENTIAL MUSHROOM OF
NUCLEAR ENERGY   23

5. THE FEDERAL GOVERNMENT AND
REAL ESTATE---GI & FHA   57

6. TRANSPORTATION   59

7. DISASTERS   65

8. DEMOCRATS ON LOCO WEED   74

9. PREAMBLE TO THE CONSTITUTION   76

10. THE IMAGINARY IMMIGRATION DEPARTMENT   78

11. TAXES UPON TAXES; CAPITAL GAINS TAX   84

12. THE SOCIAL SECURITY ACT OF 1935
AND CONGRESS   88

13. ARE YOU GETTING THE MESSAGE YET?   90

14. CONSTITUTIONAL AMENDMENTS AND
ARTICLES TO BE REVISED   94

15. PATRIOTIC POEMS   100

16. ACKNOWLEDGEMENTS   104

17. ABOUT THE AUTHOR   105

APPENDIX   109

CHAPTER 1

AMERICA THE GREATEST BUT-----

INTRODUCTION

I am writing this book because I have endured just about all I can take with Politicians, Life Time Judges, Immigration Dept., Big Oil, ACLU, Child Molesters, Drug Dealers, Air Pollution, Water Pollution, Environmentalist, and that's just for starters. The majority of Americans do not vote. They complain a lot, but not to the right people. They do not let their Senators and Representatives know what they think. This is one of the reasons our Country is in the emergency mode at the present time.

I hope you will grasp something in this book to entice you to help me make America a model of freedom for the entire world to see. Currently we are not seen as a model of democracy in many areas of the world. Even in Countries where we have spent millions of dollars for food, water, medical supplies, housing and even our military that has sacrificed thousands of lives to protect them from Dictators.

I personally do not like the way our freedom is being taken away little by little. There are groups that remind me of the way Germany was taken over by the mad man Hitler, and the way Iraq was controlled by Hussein. The American Civil Liberties Union, federal judges, some members of congress, and extreme liberals are doing their best to control the Government. We cannot allow this to happen here. As I have stated in this book, I am concerned about the direction America is headed. We must wake up people, or we are headed for the destruction of the greatest Government in the world. We cannot stand by and do nothing. This is the motivation for writing this book. If we do not make some drastic changes to the Constitution, we are in deep trouble. Thank God for Bill O'Reilly of Fox News. He is making a difference, but he needs our help. I am trying to help him because he is taking the right road. If you doubt Mr. O'Reilly's love for America, please read his book, Culture

Warrior.

The most important change to the Constitution was the amendment to allow the President of the U. S. to serve only two terms. This was very important as it eliminated a group with lots of money and power to create a Dictator so to speak.

In this book you will see that I have recommended many changes to the Constitution that I believe essential for a better Government. If I can convince you to take an active roll in Government, either by running for office or just letting your Senators know how you feel, my reward for writing this book will be priceless. I believe one issue that needs to be revised ASAP is term limits for congress. Some of these Senators have been in congress so long they forget who they are supposed to represent. With the power they have they lose sight of what is essential and important for the people. With term limits we will have representatives for the people and not for their own self interest.

Our Government is so in debt to Japan and China, it is close to financial collapse. The congress could fix this problem if they didn't waste so much on pork.

Read on my friends and if you are as irritated as I am about the way things are going in Government, together we can make a difference.

Shakespeare wrote. "All the World is a stage." Unfortunately the U.S. is not seen as the good guy star in all the acts. We must however, end up as the hero in the third act, so that all the world will applaud our performance.

British Prime Minister Tony Blair, speaking on the third anniversary of the coalition invasion of Iraq said. "What happens in Iraq or Afghanistan today is not just crucial for the people in those countries or even in those regions, but for our security here and round the world. It is an entirely noble cause to help people in need of our help in pursuit of liberty, and a self-interest one, since in their salvation is our own security."

America is at one of the most critical stages in U. S. history. There are so many

BUTS that have to be taken care of, or we will never last another two hundred years. It is imperative that we, the American citizen start paying attention, and voice opinions about issues that are slowly eroding our freedom that was mandated by the Constitution. It is very easy to contact your Representatives and Senators by E-Mail or by the blue pages in your phone book. Let all your friends on your E-Mail list know how you feel and encourage them to side with you on the issues. Your Representatives in Washington will listen, because you are the voters that put them there.

Times change very fast because some people are never satisfied with the status quo. Some are very slow because of greed, uncertainty and politics. As we reflect back on the past, these words are so true. Take a look at the advancement we have made in space exploration, medicine, DNA, gene knowledge, electronics and communications. On the negative side, we are still forced to use gasoline to operate our automobiles and pollute the air we breathe. We are polluting the air with all kinds of health problems from coal-fired electric generating plants. We are destroying the oceans and marine life with oil spills from cargo ships and drilling rigs. We are destroying the ozone layer, thereby causing the ice in the Artic to melt, thereby creating another problem. The weather pattern is changing, which in turn will create more devastating storms.

Here is a question for all you readers. Do you believe the World Trade Agreement and illegal immigration are creating a lower standard of living for the U. S. citizen? It is pre-determined that politics and greed are.

President Fox should be exceptionally proud of his foreign policy. It seems that his foreign policy is working extremely well. Most of his people have fled Mexico for the U.S. to be free and gain a decent standard of living. They will not be sending money back to Mexico if they get to stay here. They were proud citizens of your country, but have had enough of poverty, and a government that caters to a select few. That is not what democracy is all about. It seems that you and your peers think that you can get away with hoarding all the wealth. This only works for a period of time. Eventually the masses determine they have no say in the government. I'm sure it was fun for you while it lasted. Now it is time to face the consequences. Cuba and Castro would have faced the same situation if it wasn't for the Atlantic Ocean. Many Cubans have tried to flee Cuba for the U. S. in small boats and anything that would float. They even tried to cross on rafts, and risk their lives to get here. Some even lost their lives in the attempt. That's how bad they want freedom. Venezuela, Iran, Syria, North Korea and a few other Countries without freedom will wise up after it is too late. The World deserves freedom.

People will only be treated like animals for a period of time and the sooner all you Dictators wake up to this fact, the faster your country will prosper for all people.

On April 10, 2006 thousands of illegals, mostly Mexicans, demonstrated in cities across the U. S. demanding citizenship. This is deplorable, and should not be tolerated. They have broken a law, plain and simple. I feel for them; however there is a right and a wrong way to accomplish a goal. Some of the Senators are pushing for amnesty. In my judgment this is very wrong. This sends the wrong message to other countries that are faced with the same situation as Mexico. Where does it stop? Wake up Congress. What you need to do is secure our borders now. You do not provide amnesty to twenty million illegals. This is a political issue. It is time for the American Citizens to make you enforce the laws of this Country.

CHAPTER 2

AMERICA THE GREATEST BUT-----

Citizens of America this is the way I see the Government of the U. S. A. and the direction it is headed. After reading what I have to say, I sincerely hope you see it my way also. Will you help me save this great nation? It doesn't matter if you are a Democrat, Republican, Independent, Black, White, Yellow or Red, as long as you are a legal Citizen. We must come together and save this Nation.

I am negative about many things and I see need for change in this the greatest Country in the World. I intend to elaborate on many of these issues to make this an even better Country for the next two hundred years. This is the greatest Country in the World and I have proof. Can twenty million plus illegal immigrates be wrong? If you need proof, take a trip to a few of our neighboring Countries. Start with Mexico or any Central America Country, Europe, Asia, Far East, Africa. If you still don't think that the USA is the best in the World, perhaps you better pack up and move. Sure it is nice to visit and see how people in other Countries live. See their culture and scenery. It is rewarding to see The Great Wall of China, the Taj Mahal, and the great Pyramids of Egypt. Paris France is loaded with Historic places. If you don't believe me, ask the most traveled past President in U. S. history, you guessed it, William Jefferson Clinton.

The one place you will want to see after all this travel is the U.S.A. I was in the Army in WW II and spent 26 months in Europe. I was in the invasion of France at Normandy on Omaha Beach 6/6/1944. I was in France, Scotland, England, Wales, Luxembourg, and the Belgium countryside. I have vacationed with my beautiful wife Bonnie in Mexico four times; Bermuda, Hawaii, Puerto Rico, St. Martin and I have never had the desire to live any place other than the good ole USA.

If there ever was a time to take an active role in our Government it is now. Too many Americans have become complacent and have no idea what is going on, and could care less. For many as long as they can watch a good sports game, have a six pack and a big pizza they are happy. The soccer moms are too busy with the kids, shopping and housekeeping. They don't have time to even think about what is going on. This is exactly what the Politicians want. As long as the members of Congress can make you think they are doing great things for you, you will vote them in term after term, that's providing you even vote.

I for one believe that even though America is the greatest Country in the World, there are <u>many</u> things that should be changed, and the sooner the better, before it is too late. It is up to you American Citizens, to help force these changes.

Many issues are controlled by big business, politicians, labor unions, and even big money from Foreign Countries. What has happened to Government of the people, by the people and for the people? It is currently Government of the Congress, by the Congress and for the Congress. The most important critical changes to be made will require an amendment to the Constitution. This will not be easy, but it is essential for the sake of this Government in more ways than one.

I believe term limits are essential for both the House and Senate. I also believe that we should have term limits on Regional Judges, and Supreme Court Judges. To take this one step further, what is wrong with these judges being elected to office by the people?

Here is an excellent example of a Federal Judge in Vermont that gave a child molester a sentence of 60 days in jail. The guilty person had done this over a period of four years. I believe the people should have something to say about this by voting these Judges out of office. Too many Judges are using their own interpretation of the Constitution. The Judges that want to make it legal for two people of the same sex to marry. This, my friends is unacceptable and against the law.

You have witnessed on TV in 2005 and 2006 the process of appointing Supreme Court Judges. What a waste of time by the members of Congress. It is a calamity any time a new Judge has to be appointed. It is nothing except a political fight, and a waste of time and money by the Congress. It also brought out the intelligent thinking of Ted Kennedy. If he only would step back and look in the mirror, he would see how stupid he looked. In the process of writing this book, I have asked many people this question, do you think we need term limits for Congress? I have yet to have one person say no.

Do you think for one minute the likes of Teddy or Byrd, just to name two, want to forfeit that lucrative position with all the perks, pay, free travel, and that WOW pension? No way! I will not address either one of them as honorable senators when they have no respect for the office of the President, especially during time of war. All they are doing is telling the enemy that they do not agree with what the President is doing. Both of these senators should be censured by the congress. It is difficult to understand why the voters in Mass. and West Virginia keep voting these two individuals into office. Did you get as irritated as I did when Ted Kennedy called President Bush a liar? I guess the Chappaquiddick incident slipped his mind. For all the younger generation who never heard of Chappaquiddick on 7/16/1969, See next chapter.

TED KENNEDY AND CHAPPAQUIDDICK

Here is a brief summary of what took place. Every summer, the Edgartown Yacht Club sponsored the Edgartown Regatta off Martha's Vineyard. The Kennedy's had been attending the regatta for years, and their celebrations were the stuff of legend. Two Kennedy boats, the Resolute and the Victura, were entered in the 1969 races.

Bobby's former campaign staff, consisting of Mary Jo Kopechne, Rosemary Keough, Esther Newberg, Susan Tannenbaum, Nance Lyons, and Mary Ellen Lyons, were invited for the weekend festivities. Naturally a lot of drinking was going on. Ted hooked up with Mary Jo Kopechne and was to take her back to the landing to catch the Ferry back to Edgartown. In the process he accidentally, with the help of a few drinks too many, drove off the dike bridge into Poucha Pond. The car turned upside down and Kennedy somehow was able to get out and swim to shore. He later testified that he dived down until exhausted trying to get Mary Jo out of the car. He then proceeded to walk back to where the rest of his friends were. Ted suggested to his longtime friend that he tell the authorities that Mary Jo was driving and was alone. After nine hours of sobering up, Ted finally reported the accident. After all that elapsed time there was no way the Police could determine if he had any alcohol in his blood.

All kinds of scenarios took place during the investigation, the trial and the testimony. However with the Kennedy influence and money, poor Teddy got off with a slap on the hand. The Citizens of Massachusetts should be outraged and ashamed to be represented by this Senator.

Sure America is great because we have freedom. Freedom of speech, religion, press, to bear arms, have council, but have you noticed, a few minorities, with the help of some liberal Federal District Judges are trying to take away some of our freedoms? This has to be stopped, and one way to stop it is to demand that these appointed Judges be stripped of their authority. Do you agree that District Judges should be appointed for life or be elected by the voters to serve two terms? You have no doubt noticed that the press also has gone beyond their authority a few times with their reporting. I have seen on television CBS, CNN, and others of giving troop movements, where, when and how many. The New York Times holds the record for taking the first amendment to the point of treason. I'm talking about the information on the front page of the N. Y. Times about the U. S. tracking money transfers from banks to the Terrorist.

If this type of reporting had been allowed during the invasion of France at Normandy on 6/6/1944, the Germans would have been ready, and the invasion would have been a disaster and a total failure. This, my friends is called freedom of the press by many. I think it borders on treason. What do you think? The First Amendment gives every Citizen the right to free speech. The ranting and raving of Ted Kennedy and Jane Fonda give new meaning to the term free speech. Oh yes, don't forget slick Willie Clinton. This is another dumb mistake he made in 2006 in a speech when he told Arab students at a forum at the American University of Dubai, United Arab Emirates, that "the U. S. made a big mistake when it invaded Iraq. Saddam is gone. It's a good thing, but I don't agree with what was done."

Well as I have stated in this book, during Clintons term in office, and all the terrorist attacks on the U.S., he did nothing. So are you surprised? In case Willie doesn't know it, I think his buddy-buddy time with the Elder Bush is a thing of the past. Does this kind of a speech look like a past President Rhodes Scholar to you?

AMENDMENTS TO THE CONSTITUTION

In my opinion, the first amendment should be amended to read that giving solace, comfort, hope, or building the morale of the enemy is considered treason. Traitor Fonda got away with her escapade during the Viet-Nam war. Let her not get away with our war with the Terrorist. If she mouthed that kind of treason in Great Britain, Tony Blair would have her deported. I think she should be deported to a Ben Laden cave in Afghanistan, Viet Nam, North Korea, or some remote Island.

She is a disgrace to this Country and should be stripped of her Citizenship. She is such a disgrace that Ted Turner couldn't even stand to live with her. And you don't get much more liberal than he is. I can hear the Hollywood liberals now complaining about the right to say anything they wish. Free speech is not free. It is very costly, especially in time of war. Even the press and television commentators have a tendency to go too far in reporting the news by relating some of their own personal thoughts in the process. Many times they hurt our cause or put our troops in harms way by too much information like dates, time and where our army will be. Dan Rather of CBS went a little too far on some unsubstantial news, and was forced to retire.

WORLD WAR II

In 1940 and 1941, 80 to 90% of Americans did not want to go to war to help Great Britain who was fighting to save their Country from the mad man Hitler who was responsible for killing millions of Jews as well as millions of other people who got in his way and millions wounded. Just like in present time, many Americans did not want to go to war with Iraq. Did they think for one minute that the flying of planes into the World Trade Center buildings was not war? So you counter by saying Iraq had nothing to do with Bin Laden.

Do you believe that flight 800 was shot down by a rocket on July 17, 1996? Well I think it was, and I don't care what excuse the Government used for the reason. I have searched the Web for more information on flight 800 and it is very apparent that the reason for the crash was not what the Federal Governments agreed on as a final conclusion.

Flight 800 Independent Researchers Organization: See appendix: page 109.

Think what could have happened if the Government of the United States had not made Japan so angry they decided to wage war against us. The sneak attack by the Japanese Navy and Air Force on Sunday, December 7, 1941 against the U. S. Navel Fleet anchored in Pearl Harbor, Hawaii and the Army Barracks in Honolulu devastated our navy fleet and killed thousands of Navy and Army personnel. The attack caught the U. S. by complete surprise and many of our fighter planes were destroyed before they could even take off from the air fields to fight back. Of course President Roosevelt declared war on Japan and as soon as Hitler heard the news, he declared war on the USA. This forced us into WW II and the rest is history.

WW II brought out the pinnacle of patriotism beyond any war, except perhaps the American Revolution. Americans were united and willing to do whatever it took to win the war. Our Navy was almost destroyed in the bombing of Pearl Harbor on Sunday December 7, 1941. Our military was in no way ready to attack or defend, for that matter, any major battle.

Patriotism was so high many men, some not even 18 years old, voluntarily signed up for various branches of the military. Many women joined various branches of the service and many went to work in factories helping to build military equipment. This country was not ready for any major conflict, but was up and ready for the invasion of France just two years and six months after Pearl Harbor.

If you want this Country to survive another two hundred years, you better get mad, get tough and help make our Government join the 21st Century. I am going to point out the changes that I think are essential for America to remain the greatest Country in the World for all future years to come. I will start with the highest Office in our Government, the President and will explore the changes that I believe will really excite your thinking about the members of the House and Senate, the Supreme Court Judges and the District Judges who are appointed for life. As mentioned earlier in regard to District Judges, they should be elected and not appointed. I believe it is essential that the Supreme Court Judges also should be elected by the citizens. Why? Did you happen to catch the ritual by the Congress Committee conducting the interrogation of Judge Samuel Alito for the position on the Supreme Court on TV? This political appointment by the President is ridiculous, a waste of time and money. Also it is so ridiculous that many Judges who are highly qualified will not even consider the job. Would you want to hear the nonsense spewed out of the likes by Ted Kennedy again, again and again? We the people are very capable of electing a Judge for the Supreme Court and I have said previously, it will not be for life. Do you think we are getting the most brilliant and qualified Judges wanting to be on the Supreme Court? Well I don't because they do not want to be questioned for 18 or 20 hours by a panel of Congressmen who are only interested in politics. If we are capable of electing a President, the highest office in the U. S., I believe we can handle electing a Supreme Court Justice. The new elected Judges would be allowed to serve two terms of 6 years. If after sitting out for 12 years, they want to run for an additional 2 terms, this would be allowed. No Judge would be allowed to serve past the age of 82 and this includes Federal District Judges. Election of Supreme Court Judges would be three every two years. This, my friends, is just the tip of the Iceberg.

YOU HAVE THE POWER:

You may have at your disposal one of the most potent weapons right in your home, it is called a computer. With this computer you have the power to force changes in the way laws are made and the way Congress does business. It is past time to let these Politicians know that they are in Washington to represent the people and not their own self interest. Do you know how many voters will agree with you? If you have ten people on your E Mail list, and they have at least ten on their list, this number mushrooms into thousands very quickly, and that my friends, is noticed in Washington. If you let your Senators and Representatives know that you are paying attention, they will pay attention. Do you realize you can see how they vote on the issues from your potent weapon, and even on some TV stations? Don't just get mad and complain to your friends, complain to your Senators and Representatives in Washington. Just go to your computer or call them on your cell phone. They are all available on your computer by e-mail and in the blue pages of your phone book if you don't have a computer.

If I haven't inspired you to help me make these changes, this Country is headed for a disastrous fall of the greatest Government the World has ever known. I have a basis for this belief. This Country is being taken over by minorities, environmentalist, Government Judges, people who want GOD out of everything, and just plain Citizens who pay no attention to what is taking place. We need to get District Judges out of power who are letting these things happen. The ACLU is actually American Civil Liberties Union. They are doing everything they can to take away our freedom. The only freedom they want is what will benefit them. Kind of reminds you of the way Hitler took over Germany. Read Culture Warrior, by Bill O'Reilly if you want to see what is going on in America.

ENVIRONMENTALIST

The Environmentalist would rather see thousands of acres of forest destroyed, and the burning of houses, fireman injured and killed, thousands of dollars spent fighting fires rather than trees harvested systematically. All that has to be done to keep this disaster from happening is to cut enough trees to make a fire break. Just this one minor thing could save thousands of acres of forest. Don't you think it would be better than the stupidity of some to choose the other way? Wake up Environmentalist. You can't see the forest for the smoke. The one thing I agree with the Environmentalist on is objecting to drilling for oil in Alaska. However I disagree for a different reason than they do. I want the government to push for the hydrogen cell cars, and we won't need so much oil. Senator Richard Lugar from Indiana is doing his part trying to wean the U. S. from oil. You Environmentalist are always wanting to make a difference, now is the time to shine. In order to save this Planet, you better put the heat on Congress to wean the U S from oil, coal and nuclear as energy. It is very obvious that emission from the use of these fuels are destroying the ozone, and creating Global Warming. The Polar Ice Caps are melting, which causes the Oceans to warm up. This is responsible for more hurricanes, and storms. It also increases the ocean level to rise, which will cause more erosion, destroy property close to the beaches and some Islands will be completely covered. This is a matter not to be taken lightly. The people who want to make it legal for two people of the same sex to marry. The Government itself, that is governed by a Judicial, Legislative, and Executive Branch that has too much power and is desperately in need of change. The greedy CEO's of large Companies who spend their time trying to figure how to rip off the stock holders and line their own pockets rather than helping the very people who helped them to become successful. It is past time for the Government to pass some laws on Corporate Management to insure that they cannot sell any stock they possess without a thirty day written notice to sell and proof of solvency of the company, to the Chairman of the Security and Exchange Commission; only then with a written notice of approval from the Chairman of the SEC. This ruling will be in effect for any member of the

Company board of Directors who want to sell in excess of 5000 shares in less than 30 days. Management will not be allowed to borrow funds from the Corporation without approved by the board of directors by secret ballot; and then only with proof of adequate collateral, stock not included. To make it more secure, all Company CEO's and Board Members stock will be held by the SEC.

THE CLINTON YEARS

The first major topic I am going to address is the Oval Office. I said Oval Office, not the evil office. However it has been evil by many past Presidents.

During the Clinton administration, the one of many things that got my blood pressure up was the power that he had legally. Something no President should ever have. In the last minutes of his term in office, he had the authority to pardon criminals that had been convicted of a crime by a legal trial and jury and sentenced by a Judge. Actually he was to obtain information from the Attorney General before deciding to pardon any of them, but he did not and used his own discretion. This is blatant injustice by thumbing his nose at the legal system of the United States of America. I don't care if he had the right to do this, or not, but it is wrong and has to be stopped. Would you believe the reason just could be because Mark Rich had millions? Mrs. Rich wasn't bad to look at either. I'm sure slick Willie noticed this.

Another example of his legal power was the record breaking amount spent on travel to foreign Countries. We will never know the exact total but it was $95,000,000 up to 1995. Thanks to Clinton, a cap should be put on travel by the President, and Congress should approve any amount over that cap, on an annual basis.

The President's foreign travel is well reported, but its cost is largely unavailable. Because this president has set records as the most traveled president in American history, three U.S. Senators requested the government's official auditor to examine some of his recent travel expenses he incurred. Senate Republican Policy Committee Chairman Larry Craig, and Senators Jeff Sessions and Craig Thomas last year requested the General Accounting Office to examine the costs of just three recent trips taken by President Clinton in 1998-his travel to Chile, China, and to six countries in Africa. The results of this study, released by the General Accounting Office, suggested that Clinton's travel has gone past the level of excessive to that of abusive.

Just those three trips cost the American taxpayer at least $72 million-with the Africa trip alone accounting for $42.8 million. Not only did they seriously affect the taxpayer's wallet, these three trips seriously affected America's defense. Fully 84 percent of the $72 million price tag came from the (DOD) Department of Defense budget. For example, the cost per hour to fly Air Force One, the president's personal plane, is $34,400. Of course, the $72-million price tag paid for a lot more than just flying President Clinton. It also paid for 297 military missions largely for the ferrying back and forth of some 2,400 people and necessary equipment working sometimes months in advance to assure smooth travel for the President.

The trip to Africa alone involved 10 advance trips by military planes and the travel of 904 DOD personnel-the equivalent of a U.S. Army battalion. As costly as the tab for these three presidential trips was, it does not measure the full cost to the taxpayer. GAO (General Accounting Office) did not tabulate the additional costs of President Clinton's security out-of-country expenses these were not requested for security purposes. Neither was the agency planning expenses included. Nor did GAO add in the cost of paying the military and other personnel who accompanied or prepared the way for President Clinton (despite the economic fact that these personnel would have been doing some other job if not on travel.) Rather, only the additional, or "incremental," cost that the President's travel entailed is represented by the GAO figures. It is, then, by any description a conservative estimate.

At the same time that President Clinton was using the Pentagon as his personal travel agent, he was also cutting back its budget. Every year he was in office,

President Clinton cut the military budget. It is not an exaggeration to say that President Clinton's travel has been excessive:

He already holds countless records for presidential foreign travel-Most Countries visited (59), Total foreign travel days (186), and most days of foreign travel per year (27.6).

A synopsis of GAO's report follows;

The one I loved the most was helping him pay for his little jaunt to see the Taj Mahal. He didn't make any excuse for going, except to say, "It has been my lifelong dream ever since I was a little boy to see the Taj Mahal." On his trip through the India subcontinent it was noted that several helicopters were used to shuttle his daughter Chelsea and a group of her friends around. Hillary did not go on this trip but her Mother did. Clinton could have seen a lot of sights if he had gone into the military instead of rushing off to England to avoid the draft. How could anybody in the military look up to a Commander In Chief that left the Country to avoid serving his Country.

Thank God for the 22nd Amendment. It called for term limits for the President. Without term limits Clinton would still be in Office and the Terrorist would be all over us. Look at his record on Bin Laden.

Feb. 1993 World Trade Center bombed by Muslim fanatics, killing six people and injuring hundreds. Clinton did nothing.

Oct. 1993 eighteen American soldiers killed in Somalia. Body of one was dragged through the streets of Mogadish as hordes of Somalians cheered. Clinton responded by calling off the hunt for Mohanned Farrah Aidid and ordered Troops home.

Oct. 1995 five Americans killed and thirty wounded by a car bomb in Saudi Arabia set by Muslin extremists. Clinton did nothing.

JUNE 1996 U.S. Air Force housing complex in Saudi Arabia bombed by Muslin Extremists. Clinton did nothing.

Nov. 1997 Iraq refused to allow U. N. weapon inspectors do their jobs and threatened to shoot down U S spy planes. Clinton did nothing.

Feb 1998 Clinton threatened to bomb Iraq but called it off when the U N said no.

Aug 7 1998 U. S. Embassies in Kenya and Tanzania were bombed by Muslin Extremist. Clinton did nothing.

Aug 20 1998 Monica appeared for third time to testify before grand jury. Clinton countered by bombing Afghanistan and Sudan, damaging a camel and an aspirin factory.

Dec 16 1998 House of Representatives proposed to impeach Clinton the next day.

Clinton countered by ordering major air strike against Iraq, described by the New York Times as, by far the largest military action in Iraq since the end of the Gulf War in 1991.

Oct. 2000 U.S. Cole bombed by Muslin Extremists, killing several U. S. sailors. Clinton did nothing.

NEWS FLASH JUST OUT; Indianapolis Star Sunday 7-18-04

What should have been front page news, buried center of page A 4, titled 1998 Intelligence Report told of suspected Bin Laden plot. Poor Liberals, now they can't blame President Bush for 9-11.

If you need more proof about the Clintons during their term in the White House, read the book Unlimited Access, by Gary Aldrich. Gary was an FBI Agent in the White House during Clinton's term as President. The Clinton's tried to stop publication of the book, but to no avail. The book was a New York Times best seller. After you read this book and you still want Hillary Clinton as President, you need to seek medical attention. Is this who you want as Commander in Chief of all the U.S. Armed Forces?

CHAPTER 3

ECONOMY INDEPENDENCE OR BANKRUPTCY

Do you know who is and what is controlling the economy in this Country? If you answered the Federal Reserve chairman, you are wrong. If you answered Congress or the President, you are still wrong. What one factor dictates the upward spiral of prices on everything we need or do? If you answered oil, I give you an A +. It is now February 02/ 2005 and the Fed is talking about raising the interest rate to slow down inflation. Guess who caused inflation in this instance? You are so sharp, it is Big Oil.

BIG OIL AND THE ECONOMY:

Yes Virginia, there is a Dictator in this Country, and it is Big Oil, or Greed, take your choice. The Oil Giants control the price of oil perhaps with the aid of some politicians, and that my friend is why the United States Airlines are going bankrupt.

So fasten your seat belts because the greedy Oil Giants are forcing Americans on a bumpy ride of higher prices and one person cannot do a darn thing about it because we are forced to use their product. Some people blame 9/11, some blame the President, especially the Liberals, as expected. Well Folks, I blame you, me, and the rest of the Citizens of this great Country for allowing the big Oil Barrens to get away with it.

It is way past time to take action. We need to phone, write, E Mail and contact our Senators and Representatives in Washington and demand action. We are not only fighting Terrorist, Big Oil is a threat to this country. Let us focus again on our so-called oil rich friends in Saudi Arabia. What would you do if you were in control of Saudi Arabia and you witnessed the happy smiles on the faces of the people in Iraq going to vote for the first time in thirty years, free from a Tyrant, and warned by the Insurgents that they would be killed if they even attempted to vote. Would you believe that a larger percentage went to the polls to vote under those conditions than the American Citizens did in our last Presidential election? If Democracy is so embraced in Iraq, is Saudi Arabia far behind? If you could see your private little money making scheme tumbling down barrel by barrel, wouldn't you be trying to stop it? Big Oil has to be reined in. Congress has to take the necessary steps to put a stop to this price gauging. If Bill Gates of Microsoft had a monopoly, what does that make Exxon Mobile? Do you know that Exxon Mobile made a net profit of one Billion dollars in 2004? You think that's greed? Look at ten Billion in 2005. Profit in 2006 is well on its way to be much larger yet. I think the Government should give the Oil Companies a big tax break, don't you?

Due to the Oil Companies greed and high prices on fuel, thousand of people have lost their jobs in the Airline industry. The Airlines cut back on the number of flights, and took some major cities off service altogether. ATA according to a report in the Indianapolis Star 02/19/05 by Ted Evanoff, fuel cost rose by $146 million, which caused profits to dry up last year. Its Executives have insisted soaring fuel costs contributed to its bankruptcy. With a war going on in Iraq, is Big Oil helping our cause? I think they should be ashamed of themselves.

I think Big Oil is in bed with Saudi Arabia. Together they are controlling the production of oil to drive up prices. And as a little reminder, don't forget that most of the Terrorist that waged war on the U.S. by destroying the World Trade Center and killing thousand of people were from Saudi Arabia.

I also put the blame on our Government Officials because I know and you know Big Oil has dollars of influence on many government people in Office. If they didn't, we wouldn't be dependent on oil for gasoline for our cars and trucks today. When the Hydrogen Cell Cars and Trucks take over, and we no longer need to depend on foreign oil, how long do you think it will be before the Oil producing countries start begging the U.S. to send them food for their starving people? We all know that only a few select people reap the windfall off of oil sales in the Dictator Controlled Countries. This is also true in Mexico, which is one reason for their Citizens rushing to the U.S. If

Democracy is not embraced as the form of government in these Countries, civil unrest will always be the norm.

Another theory why oil prices are so high is because a group of people with plenty of money and energy traders in New York and London are fixing the prices. This is manipulating the market to drive up the price of oil. This causes inflation and will ruin the economy. This in turn will demoralize the American public and the blame will go to the President because he is from a big oil state. Even though President Bush cannot run again for the Office, the Republicans will be blamed and guess what Liberal will be President? Is it going to be Hillary? You better hope not, or we will be going down the tube even faster than we are already. Can you vote for a person with her past questionable history to be the Commander in Chief of all the U.S. Armed Forces? If she is elected, she can finally have her own Plantation and Willie can be in charge of the Maids.

CEO'S ARE RIPOFF ARTIST:

Executives of Enron, Tyco, World Com, and many other greedy companies thus far have not received their just penalties. As of this date, 03/15/05 former CEO Bernard Ebbers of world Com was convicted of engineering the largest corporate fraud in U. S. history; an $11 billion accounting scandal that capsized the big telecom company three years ago. A Federal jury in Manhattan returned guilty verdicts on all nine counts, including securities fraud, conspiracy and lying to regulators, a decision that could send Ebbers, age 63, to prison for the rest of his life.

What I want to know and I'm sure you do too, when is the Government going to bring charges against Kenneth Lay, CEO of Enron? If he is found guilty of fraud, and it sure looks that way, he should be stripped of all his assets and be incarcerated.

All the money from the sale of his assets, and he has plenty, should be turned over to the Stock Holders. Well it has finally happened. Kenneth Lay and former CEO Jeffery Skilling have been brought to trial as of 02/2006. It will be weeks before they have a verdict. As of March 17, 2006, the trial against Kenneth Lay was not going in favor of the Stockholders. The testimony of Chief Financial Officer Andrew Fastow was not very incriminating against CEO Kenneth Lay, and former CEO Jeffery Skilling. However, with a surprise witness, a former Enron accountant, Sherron Watkins, testified for the prosecution and had some very damming evidence. If Mr. Lay and Mr. Skilling are found guilty, they should get the maximum penalty. Granted, a lot of Stockholders lost their life savings to these ripoff artist. Now these two are small fish compared to the CEO'S of the big oil CEO'S. They are ripping off every citizen in the United States and the Government is doing nothing about it.

News flash:

CEO Kenneth Lay passed away July 5, 2006 from a heart attack. He had not been sentenced by the Court, so now the Stockholders will have to bring Civil Charges against his personal assets.

MILLIONS SPENT ON THE WRONG PLANET:

The U.S. spends millions on space exploration and it has led to some amazing discoveries. What blows my mind is the fact that we can go the Moon and back, send a Rover to Mars, guide it around, take pictures that can be transmitted back to Earth, but we can't operate a car on anything but gasoline. We have been told that it is possible to operate a car on hydrogen cells, so what is the hold up? The Japanese have already come up with a Hybrid car that runs on battery and gasoline. Japan is totally dependent upon imported oil, so they had to find a way to keep from using as much oil as possible. The Hybrid car fills that need to a certain extent, but not completely. The Hybrid gets about twice the mileage on a gallon of gas as the all gasoline car. The Japanese are working on a Hydrogen Cell car that omits nothing from the exhaust but water, and requires no gasoline. The Japanese have forced the American automobile companies to start making Hybrids in order to be competitive. Presently the American Government is saying that it will be at

21

least ten years before we will have Hydrogen Cell cars that will be affordable. In case you didn't know it, the Government has been testing cars and buses with Hydrogen cells in Washington D.C. for the past two years. I believe the Japanese will force the American gasoline cars off the roads when they come out with their Hydrogen Cell cars. The only reason we have not progressed to obsolescence on the gasoline engine is because of the Oil Giants. The British already have a high pressure hydrogen fuel cell motorcycle. Germany and Iceland have hydrogen cell cars.

Big Oil will want to control the distribution of the hydrogen. Not only will this be cheaper if the Government keeps the oil companies out of this market, but they will have to keep control of the price. Can you imagine the cleaner air to breathe again? The only emission is water. Keep the heat on the Government for oil free transportation.

CHAPTER 4

THE SHOCKING TRUTH ABOUT THE ELECTRIC UTILITIES AND THE POTENTIAL MUSHROOM OF NUCLEAR ENERGY

Yes, it is nice to have instant light at the touch of a switch. The many Appliances, tools, and thousands of conveniences all operated by electricity, but at what price?

As the American people witness almost on a daily basis, the inability of the Electric Utilities to provide uninterrupted service because of storms, floods, accidents, blown transformers, fires as a result of faulty wiring, lines down because the lines and poles are subject to wind, trees falling across lines and a hundred other reasons. This makes you wonder how they ever got a patent in the first place. Well in the first place, very little was known about electricity. It was going to replace the gas lights and that was good. It since has expanded to encompass the daily lives of every citizen in the U. S. A. Do you think the Electric Utilities might have a problem getting a patent today? How many deaths do you think Electricity is responsible for? How about deaths from coming in contact with high voltage lines, and from fires caused by shorts? We all have witnessed what happens in a Hurricane in Florida. Thousands, even millions, are without power for days and sometimes even weeks. The landscape is ruined by unsightly giant towers of 97,000 miles of power lines across the Nation. Electric poles dot the Cities, Towns and across the Countryside. Radiation emitted from high voltage power lines may be hazardous to your health. The results of tests are either not conclusive or as yet not released. A friend of mine drove through a housing addition with his Geiger counter turned on, and he said it went crazy because of the high tension power lines on giant towers that ran across the addition. What are the Electric Utilities doing to correct the numerous safety problems they have, and the ability to keep the Citizens from interrupted service during storms. The only thing I see them doing is spending Dollar after Dollar on

TV ads to warn people to stay away from high voltage power lines.

I was in Florida in October 2004 shortly after the hurricanes and was chatting with an Employee of a Cracker Barrel about the damage from the Hurricanes. She mentioned that a large group of Electric Repairmen had been in the Restaurant for meals and she asked one of them why they didn't bury the lines to keep from having service interrupted every time their was a storm. He immediately replied that it would cost too much. She told him it might be cheaper than repairing over and over after every storm.

NUCLEAR ENERGY AND COAL FIRED POWER PLANTS

Very little has been done since that first light bulb, to improve the safety and delivery of Electricity. Some Executives I'm sure will argue this fact. Some may say look how far we have come, we even have Nuclear Power. Yes, we do and I for one believe all of these plants should be shut down immediately and made safe from radiation. This is just a tragedy waiting to happen. There is no way these plants can be protected from the terrorist

Do you recall what happened in an explosion of a Nuclear Power Station in Chernobyl, Russia? An explosion killed 31 people in the world's worst disaster. Many more will die, 16,000 estimated, in coming years due to radiation exposure. A Terrorist attack on one of our Nuclear Power Stations, especially in the Western United States would kill millions of Citizens. I think Chernobyl was a lot worse than the general public ever knew about as it was downplayed because of our own Nuclear Power Stations.

ENERGY PLANT POLLUTION

Now note this from The Indianapolis Star by John Heilprin of Associated Press. The government agreed Thursday to decide by this summer whether it should force coal-fired power plants in 13 states, including Indiana, to reduce unhealthy air pollution blamed for obscuring views of the Smokey Mountains. North Carolina's attorney general, Roy Cooper, asked the Environmental Protection Agency last March to find that pollution coming from outside North Caroline was preventing the state from meeting federal health-based standards for smog and soot in metropolitan areas.

The EPA missed the November deadline for replying. But it reached a settlement with Cooper and the New York-based Environmental Defense after both filed notice of potential legal action against the EPA.

That proposed settlement was filed Thursday in U. S. District Court in Raleigh, N. C.

The state and the environmental group contend that pollution from the out-of-state plants is affecting North Carolina by harming people's health, damaging farmer's crops and distracting from mountain views that are part of its $12.6 billion-a-year tourist industry.

"This is a win for all of us who want to stop these out-of-state polluters from damaging the air we breathe," Cooper said. North Carolina is working hard to clean up our own air, but those efforts alone won't stop the dirty air we inherit from other states.

If the EPA agrees with North Carolina, coal-burning power plants upwind would have three years to cut pollution in Alabama, Georgia, Illinois, Indiana, Kentucky, Maryland, Michigan, Ohio, Pennsylvania, South Carolina, Tennessee, Virginia and West Virginia.

ELECTRICITY IS INTERRUPTED AGAIN

The Indianapolis Star, April 13, 04 read. A brief electrical outage apparently caused by a bird on a power line knocked out electricity to the Los Angeles International Airport control tower and disrupted air traffic Monday morning. Eighty to 100 flights had to hold in the air, circle or stay on the ground at other airports, Federal Aviation Administration spokesman Donn Walker said. Some departures from Los Angeles were also delayed.

Now although that is bad, it's nothing compared to the ripple effect of a tree in Ohio, brushing, not falling, against a 345,000-volt line on a hot August day in 2003, wiping out electricity for 50 million people in the Eastern United States and Canada. It cost the United States economy more than $10 billion and endangered lives.

THIS JUST IN 3/11/05; Indianapolis Star. EPA rule tightens standards on smog. Indiana's coal fired plants must make deep reductions in heart and lung-damaging pollution under federal rules signed Thursday aimed at cleaning the air Hoosiers breath and reducing pollution that drifts to other states.

Twenty-eight states in the Midwest, East and South are affected by the U.S. Environmental Protection Agency rule, which will cut nitrogen oxides, a primary component in smog, and sulfur dioxide, which forms microscopic particles. Indiana and Ohio are the Midwest's biggest polluters because of the concentration of coal-fired power plants, EPA officials said.

In terms of health and environment benefits, this ranks right up there with (reductions) in acid rain and (banning) leaded gasoline," said Bharat Mathur, acting administrator in EPA's Region 5, which includes Indiana.

By 2015, Indiana emissions of sulfur dioxide should be cut by 452,000 tons, or 56 percent, and emissions of nitrogen oxides should drop by 177,000 tons, or 68 percent, according to EPA estimates.

Nationally, the reductions are expected to prevent 17,000 premature deaths, 22,000 nonfatal heart attacks and 700,000 cases of respiratory ailments, EPA Officials said. They also will generate more than $100 billion a year in health and environmental benefits, "25 times the cost of implementing the rule," Mathur said.

EPA officials estimate achieving the pollution cuts will end up costing about $4 billion a year.

Utilities are expected to pass costs on to consumers. Cinergy's PSI Energy rates, for example, will increase an estimated average of 3 percent annually From 2005 through 2009, spokeswoman Angeline Protogere said.

Brian Wright of the Hoosier Environmental Council said he was disappointed that the rule didn't require Indiana plants to cut sulfur dioxide even further. Microscopic particles created by the pollution can lodge deep in the lungs and lead to heart and lung problems.

"The (rule) doesn't get the job done for Indiana," Wright said. "Given the known health impacts from particulate matter, which are growing as more studies come out, it's inconceivable" that the reductions aren't greater.

The federal agency has said 24 Indiana counties violate limits for ground-level ozone, and 14 counties and portions of five others violate limits on particles.

Indiana's coal-fired utilities contribute to particle pollution in 10 other states: Alabama, Georgia, Illinois, Kentucky, Michigan, North Carolina, Ohio, Penn., Tenn., and West Virginia. They contribute to ground-level ozone, or smog, in Michigan, Ohio, and Wisconsin.

While the United States is cutting its emissions, some nations, especially China, are belching out more dirty air. As a result, overseas pollution could cancel out improvements in U.S. air quality that have cost billions of dollars. Among the efforts that could be undermined: the Environmental Protection Agency's new effort to cut power plants' emissions of ozone-forming chemicals and particle pollution, specks of chemicals that damage health.

INDIVUAL HOUSEHOLD UNITS

I support individual units designed for each household or business consisting of hydrogen cell technology, solar powered, or some other free standing power unit that is safe and environmentally pure. This will solve all the problems that we currently experience with electricity.

PRESIDENT BUSH SPEECH:

Hold the presses, this just in as of 6/23/05. President Bush has stated that it is time to build more nuclear power plants. He also stated that nuclear power could play a big role in the Nations dependence on foreign fuels.

I assume he meant oil. I know they use coal which is a large portion of pollution. They have started using natural gas but it is getting to be more expensive. Nuclear power plants do generate electricity without emitting pollutants, although they create radioactive waste which may be even worse. So is this a good trade off? There is just one minor little problem dealing with this waste, which contains the used fuel rods, contain the radioactive waste. Finding a safe place to store them where they will be secure from Terrorist is a big problem. This only lasts for Centuries, so what's the big deal? Bush and other advocates of the new nuclear power say there is reduced risk of a radioactive problem. Notice the word "reduced". As far as I'm concerned, we still have a radioactive problem. Mr. Bush goes on to say, "people have got to understand that advances in science and engineering, along with plant design have made nuclear power far safer. In the previous sentence notice two words, "far safer".

This means it is still not safe, so why spend millions of dollars on a power that is going to be a problem? Let's say that you have a Nuclear Power Plant in every State, now that's what I call ample production capability.

However, if a tree falls across a power line, thousand or even millions are out of electricity. Now that is not what I call new technology for the better. It's the same old story, only more money is being wasted. Instead of wasting millions of dollars on nuclear power plants, why can't that money be spent perfecting hydrogen cell as an alternative power that is not held hostage to weather, birds, and humans? One that is environmental, friendly, reliable, and safe, such as individual hydrogen cell units.

Most ridiculous item to come in my mail from Cinergy is a pamphlet that tells how you can protect your valuable equipment by having the StrikeStop surge protector installed on your meter box. Now mind you this is only a one time charge of $167.76 [plus tax] added to your bill. Additionally, $1.99 will appear on your bill each month for the StrikeStop monetary coverage. Now what is wrong with this picture? In the first place Cinergy is telling me that the service that they provide is not safe. Without this protection on your meter box, lighting could cause a fire and burn your house down. Destroy your appliances, computer, TV, and etc.

In the Automobile industry if they put a car on the market with a safety problem, the Government makes them recall all those vehicles and make repairs to eliminate the danger. Why is this any different? Not only should Cinergy put this protection on all customer meters, but it should be at no cost to the consumer. How many people on fixed incomes would not be able to afford this protection? What say you Dept. of Energy? Is this an oversight by Secretary Samuel Bodman? Maybe he should check with the head of the Dept. that makes the Auto Industry correct problems that affect safety on vehicles at no cost to the public. After reading this, if you are ready to blow a fuse, I understand. I trust that these facts will help you see the light. Now do something about this situation by letting your Senators and Representatives know you want this antiquated system replaced with modern technology. (See letter, on the following page)

Harold W. Powell

Cinergy One
139 Last Fourth Street
Cincinnati, OH 45202

Dear Customer,

Are you just waiting for an electrical surge to damage your valuable electronics and appliances? No? Well, if you don't have the right surge protection, that's exactly what could happen. As manager of the StrikeStopTM surge protection program at Cinergy One, I've seen firsthand the trouble electrical surges can cause. I've worked closely with Cinergy customers like Dave King, who had a lightning strike that damaged his security system, TV and computer. This one strike cost Dave over $1,000. While surges are caused by a number of sources, the most obvious and dangerous source is lightning. Lightning-produced surges alone result in over $100 million in property damage every year in the U.S.

The good news for Mr. King is that when the next lightning storm passed through his neighborhood, he was protected. He had purchased our StrikeStop surge protection because he didn't want to risk additional damage to his equipment.

What's so special about StrikeStop? The StrikeStop surge protector is installed at the base of your meter, where it stops damaging surges before they have a chance to enter your home's electrical system. What's more, StrikeStop Monetary Coverage provides financial protection for damage to your electronics and appliances caused by surges which can enter your home but may not pass through the meter or the StrikeStop device. Destructive surges can occur over any line entering your home, including those carrying voice, data or video.

I've had tens of thousands of Cinergy customers sign up for StrikeStop protection; and I can help you protect your electronics and appliances as well. StrikeStop reduces hassles, like insurance premiums going up due to reported claims or the expense of repairing or replacing surge-damaged equipment. And I believe one of the best qualities of StrikeStop is that it's so affordable. You can protect your equipment in advance without spending a fortune. The StrikeStop surge protector is yours to own for only $6.99 a month (plus tax) for twenty-four interest-free payments, and you receive the StrikeStop Monetary Coverage for just. $1.99 a month. We even apply your payments directly to your monthly energy bill, so there's no additional check writing or postage expense.

I hope you will take advantage of this opportunity to protect your electronics and appliances. Take it from our customer, Dave King: "Since StrikeStop has been installed, I haven't had any problems. I've already told all my family and friends to order the device." Why not order your StrikeStop surge protection today by completing the enclosed self-addressed mailer or ordering online at Cinergy.com/energystore. To order by phone, please call 1.800.787.2505.

I look forward to helping you protect your valuable electronic equipment.

John Mollaun

StrikeStop Product Manager

You don't have to spend hundreds or even thousands of dollars in electronic repairs and replacements. Order your StrikeStop surge protection today at Cinergy.com/energystore or call 1.800.787.2505!

ANOTHER POLE AND WIRE UTILITY

In all fairness to the electric utilities, there is another pole and wire utility that has outlived its usefulness, thanks to satellites and cell phones that require no poles and wires. Although the telephone companies have served their Customers well for decades, all good things come to an end. (Imagine this earth without poles, and wires strung for thousands of miles all over the USA.) Not only can we converse any where on Earth by satellite, it is possible to send pictures and E Mail to our family and friends. A friend of mine was in Georgia in front of a Church where she used to go to Sunday school, and took a picture of the church with her cell phone. Called her mother in Indiana, who asked her where she was. The daughter told her mother that she was standing in front of their former church in the mountains of Georgia. She then sent the photo to her Mother by E Mail.

My Grandson is in the Army, stationed in South Korea and his girlfriend lives in Indiana. They talk to each other by cell phones almost on a daily basis. Now that is modern technology. He is now in Iraq, and they could if permitted, E-Mail and cell phone each other.

If you are old enough, can you remember back in the late twenties, early thirties, the party line telephones? If so, you can remember that maybe five, six or more families were on a telephone party line. Telephones at that time were powered by batteries as no electricity was available. Incoming calls were identified by rings. Each person on the party line had their own type of ring. It might be a short and a long ring, or it might be two shorts and one long. Any way you get the idea. The little problem with this system was that in very

31

short notice everybody on the party line soon learned who was getting a call. And it was often the queue to pick up the phone even if it wasn't your call, to hear what was going on. Since most people had no radio or newspaper to read, this was a sure way to find out what was going on.

As most people didn't care much for this lack of privacy, the telephone companies finally updated the system to private lines. Before the private lines were in place, we didn't need radio or newspapers. We had all the news we needed on the party line.

Why am I telling you about the past? Because it demonstrates that we can better ourselves with technology. In communication we once depended on the Pony Express to deliver our letters to the West Coast. Then along came the train which was much faster. Then along came the airplane. This was even faster. Along with faster messages came the Telegraph. This was really speedy. It used to take weeks to send a message across the Atlantic. And then a brilliant idea came along. Why not lay a cable across the ocean and send telegraph messages by wire. This was a major improvement in time compared to sending mail by Steam Ships. This was a major step in better business and keeping in touch with friends and Relatives in Europe.

The point I am making here is we must keep charging ahead with new technology. The Cell Phone has made the current telephone companies obsolete with all their wires and poles all over the landscape.

FLASH! April 21, 2005, ENERGY POLICY ACT OF 2005 H.R. 6

Signed by President 8/8/2005

Thanks to this bill, although it should have been completed a decade ago, we finally are getting serious about 21st century technology.

The Energy bill when implemented completely will eliminate dependency on oil, foreign or domestic. Oil cannot last forever and the sooner we do not have to depend on it the better. We will all be better off and so will the earth.

We will have fresh air to breathe again. The sky will be blue again. Let's sing a song of cheer again. Happy days are here again. Sorry, I got carried away.

First of all I want to congratulate the Authors of this bill, and the members of Congress who voted for it. And thanks to President Bush for signing the bill that puts this Country on the right track for the future. I am not saying these bills are perfect, but they are better than anything that has been done in the past hundred years for energy.

I strongly believe that every business and household should have their own individual energy source. The energy bill is supporting this type of thinking. As we have witnessed over the past several hurricanes, the present energy source is not capable of providing any protection for business or citizens.

With this bill and the Transportation Bill, the U.S. is finally going to join the 21st Century. I am enthused over the possibilities for the future. It will be a giant step into the future of our lives. This will be the largest advancement in technology since the invention of the automobile.

President Bush in his State of the Union speech on 1/31/2006 addressed the energy problems in this way.

"Keeping America competitive requires affordable energy. And here we have a serious problem. America is addicted to oil, which is often imported from unstable parts of the world. The best way to break this addition is through technology. Since 2001, we have spent $10 billion to develop cleaner, cheaper, and more reliable energy sources-and we are at the threshold of incredible advances."

"So tonight, I announce the advanced Energy Initiative-a 22-percent increase in clean-energy research-at the Department of Energy, to push for breakthroughs in two vital areas. To change how we power our homes and offices, we will invest more in zero emission coal-fired plants, revolutionary solar and wind technologies, and clean, safe nuclear energy."

"We must also change how we power our automobiles. We will increase our research in better batteries for hybrid and electric cars, and in pollution-free cars that run on hydrogen. We'll also fund additional research in cutting-edge methods of producing ethanol, not just from corn, but from wood chips and stalks, or switch grass. Our goal is to make this new kind of ethanol practical and competitive within six years."

"Breakthroughs on this and other new technologies will help us reach another great goal: to replace more than 74 percent of our oil imports from the Middle East by 2025. By applying the talent and technology of America, this Country can dramatically improve our environment, move beyond a petroleum-based economy, and make our dependence on Middle East oil a thing of the past."

I applaud President Bush on his Energy Plan, however, I disagree in regard to spending money on zero emission fired electric generating plants. We should be looking at alternate solutions to electric transmissions problems. Even if you have 100% clean air from electric generating plants, this does not solve the problem of no power any time we have a transmission line down. This happens anytime a hurricane, a high wind, tornado, comes along or a transformer blows up. We need, as I have stated before, individual power units in every house, place of business or whatever. This will eliminate a big problem of thousands of people without power for days, or even weeks.

I also disagree with building more nuclear power plants. I don't think they are safe, and they should be shut down and made safe ASAP.

SEE U.S. SENATOR DICK LUGAR OF INDIANA, SPEECH

ENERGY IS THE ALBATROSS OF U.S. SECURITY PAGE 36-56

Big Oil is on a self destruct course of rigging prices and greed. How are they going to self destruct, you ask? Here's how. In order for the average working population to make ends meet, we the people will demand that the Government put a stop to this outrageous price gouging. As you found out from President Bush's State of the Union speech, this scenario is beginning to take shape. It is about twenty years to late, but now at least with the prodding by the public, something is being done. Eventually Big Oil will not be needed. All we, the public needs to do is keep the heat on our elected officials to push for the Hydrogen cars and individual power source in every home and business.

The time frame that President Bush gave as 2025 for being dependent on foreign oil has a reason. If the timeline is 2025, what do you suspect the Oil Companies will do about income if they know the end of the line is fast approaching on big profits. You guessed right. We the consumer will be hostage to higher oil prices, not to mention we already have been, unless the Government takes control of this potential situation. It is time for the Congress and the President to have a plan to prevent this scenario from taking place. The President is allowing the Big Oil Companies time to get their act together and unload their stock, or get contracts from the Government to operate hydrogen service stations. This time frame is unacceptable and I see no reason why we can't be independent of oil within FIVE years. The U.S. has been testing cars and buses that run on hydrogen for over a year. If I had any oil related stock, which I don't, I would be selling it while the price is high. Then I would buy related stock in hydrogen technology, solar power and individual power sources for the home. The American auto industry is gasping for breath. They are on the verge of bankruptcy because of high Union wages and pensions for retired employees. They neglected to keep up with new technology in hybrid and hydrogen cell engines. Also the foreign Hybrid cars that have been on the market for the past three years can't keep up with the demand for their product. Hybrid cars have proven reliable and are much in demand. Most foreign cars are cheaper in price than American cars. It also has been proven that some foreign cars are more dependable than American cars.

Dick Lugar

U.S. Senator for Indiana

Contact: Andy Fisher • 202-224-2079 • Date: 3/13/2006

http://lugar.senate.gov • andy_fisher@lugar.senate.gov

Energy is the Albatross of U.S. National Security, Lugar says

U.S. Senate Foreign Relations Committee Chairman Dick Lugar addressed the Brookings Institution today on "U.S. Energy Security – A New Realism."

In this speech, Lugar says:

". . . energy is the albatross of U.S. national security."

". . . there is not a full appreciation of our economic vulnerability or the competition that is already occurring throughout the world."

". . . oil will become an even stronger magnet for conflict and threats of military action, than it already is."

"Geology and politics have created petro-superpowers that nearly monopolize the world's oil supply. According to PFC Energy, foreign governments control up to 77 percent of the world's oil reserves through their national oil companies. These governments set prices through their investment and production decisions, and they have wide latitude to shut off the taps for political reasons."

"Americans paid 17 percent more for energy in 2005 than in the previous year. That increase accounted for 40 percent of the rise in the consumer price index. Last November, we spent more than $24 billion on oil imports, accounting for more than a third of our trade deficit."

Lugar's new proposals in this speech include:

"The 'Energy Diplomacy and Security Act' (to be introduced this week) calls upon the Federal Government to expand international cooperation on energy issues. This bill will enhance international preparedness for major disruptions in oil supplies. A particular priority is to offer a formal coordination agreement with China and India as they develop strategic petroleum reserves. This will help draw them into the international system, providing supply reassurance, and thereby reducing potential for conflict.

"The bill would also stimulate regional partnerships in the Western Hemisphere. Most of our oil and virtually all of our gas imports come from this Hemisphere. The bill creates a Western Hemisphere Energy Forum modeled on the APEC energy working group. This would provide a badly-needed mechanism for hemispheric energy cooperation and consultation."

"Our policies should be targeted to replace hydrocarbons with carbohydrates. Obviously this is not a short-term proposition, but we can off-set a significant portion of demand for oil by giving American consumers a real choice of automotive fuel. We must end oil's near monopoly on the transportation sector, which accounts for 60 percent of American oil consumption."

"It is time for the oil companies to make E85 available to the consumer. If these companies do not take advantage of the incentives Congress has provided, I would be in favor of legislation mandating that they install E85 pumps in appropriate markets."

". . . Senator Obama and I will soon introduce a new bill that will promote other means to move these fuels into additional markets and make them more widely available for consumers.

Among many provisions, the Obama-Lugar bill would create an alternative diesel standard comparable to the renewable fuels standard that I helped put into the 2005 energy bill. It would also provide new incentives for the production of flexible fuel vehicles. We believe that U.S. national security will be served by more robust coordination of all the elements that contribute to energy security. Consequently, the bill also would establish the post of Director of Energy Security, who would answer to the President."

Lugar also calls for getting immediate federal loan guarantees for the first American cellulosic ethanol plant, which is planned for construction in Idaho. He also calls for a $35 per barrel of oil price floor.

He discusses details of the Bayh-Leiberman bill, which he is a co-sponsor.

Full text of the speech is below.

* * *

It is a privilege to deliver the inaugural speech for the Brookings Institution's 90th Anniversary Leadership Forum series. I have had the opportunity to come here to share my thoughts on a number of national security issues over the years, and your reception has always been generous. I appreciate very much receiving the invitation to speak from my good friend, Strobe Talbott, who has been a source of sound counsel for many years and who continues to provide outstanding national and international leadership.

Last August, I represented President Bush on a diplomatic mission to North Africa. The President asked me to go to Algeria and Morocco to facilitate the release of the longest-held prisoners of war in the world – 404 Moroccan soldiers, some of whom had been held since the 1970s by the Polisario Front operating out of Algeria. American diplomats had discussed their potential release, and General Jim Jones, Supreme Allied Commander Europe, had offered to transport the POWS home to their families in Morocco. After this humanitarian mission had been fulfilled, I had the opportunity, with the Administration's blessing, to continue on to Libya for meetings with Libyan officials, including Muammar Qaddafi.

While staying overnight in the Corinthia Hotel in Tripoli, overlooking the Mediterranean, I came face to face with a microcosm of the new reality of global economic life. It was impossible to walk around the hotel without meeting someone who was hoping to tap into Libya's oil reserves. The hotel was populated with representatives from China, India, and Western oil companies who were in Libya to stake out drilling or refining options for every pool of oil that the government might make available. **The world had come to the Corinthia Hotel to compete for the energy opportunities that were expected to develop with Libya's hopeful return to the international mainstream.**

I relate this anecdote to underscore how rapidly the world is changing due to the expansion of energy demand. These conclaves of modern day oil prospectors can be found wherever there are proven energy supplies and a government willing to bargain. Indeed, my delegation also saw evidence of this in natural gas-rich Algeria. **The Chinese and Indians, with one third of the world's people between them, know that their economic future is directly tied to finding sufficient energy resources to sustain their rapid economic growth. They are negotiating with anyone willing to sell them an energy lifeline.**

The Shifting Balance of Realism

The gasoline price spikes following the Katrina and Rita hurricanes underscored for Americans the tenuousness of short-term energy supplies. But, as yet, **there is not a full appreciation of our economic vulnerability or the competition that is already occurring throughout the world.**

In a remarkable moment during the State of the Union Address, President Bush caught the attention of the nation with five words: "America is addicted to oil." Those five words probably generated more media commentary than all the rest of his remarks from that evening combined. I had an opportunity soon after the speech to talk to the President about energy, and he admitted that he had not anticipated the impact of that statement or that some commentators would find it incongruous. I believe he is genuine in wanting to devote more focus to pursuing alternative energy sources. But his Texas roots, his administration's high-profile advocacy of opening up the Arctic National Wildlife Refuge to drilling, and other associations with the oil industry have created long-standing public impressions that the President is an oil-man who believes in the oil economy.

Though not hostile to alternative energy sources, the Bush administration clearly downplayed their significance during the early part of his presidency. Vice President Cheney, who oversaw Bush Administration energy policy, stated on April 30, 2001, "Years down the road, alternative fuels may become a great deal more plentiful than they are today. But we are not yet in any position to stake our economy and our way of life on that possibility. For now, we must take the facts as they are.

Whatever our hopes for developing alternative sources and for conserving energy - and that's part of our plan - the reality is that fossil fuels provide virtually 100 percent of our transportation needs and an overwhelming share of our electricity requirements. For years down the road, this will continue to be true."

For decades, the energy debate in this country has pitted so-called pro-oil realists against idealistic advocates of alternative energy. The pro-oil commentators have attempted to discredit alternatives by saying they make up a tiny share of energy consumed and that dependence on oil is a choice of the marketplace. They assert that our government can and should do little to change this.

They have implied that those who have bemoaned oil dependency do not understand that every energy alternative comes with its own problems and limitations. Lee Raymond, the former CEO of Exxon offered an example of this line of reasoning in 2005: "There are many alternative forms of energy that people talk about that may be interesting. But they are not consequential on the scale that will be needed, and they may never have a significant impact on the energy balance. To the extent that people focus too much on that — for example, on solar or wind…— what they are doing is diverting attention from the real issues. And 25 years from now, even with double-digit growth rates, they will still be less than 1 percent of the energy supplied to meet worldwide demand. I am more interested in staying focused on the 99 percent than the 1 percent."

Indeed, advocates of alternative energy must resist the rhetorical temptations to suggest that energy problems are easily solved. They are not. Relieving our dependence on oil in any meaningful way is going to take much greater investments of time, money, and political will. There is no silver bullet solution. But the difficulty of solving the problem does not make it any less necessary. The President's State of the Union address indicates that he understands this.

Whether or not one classifies America's oil dependence as an addiction, the bottom line is that with less than 5 percent of the world's population, the United States consumes 25 percent of its oil. If oil prices remain at $60 a barrel through 2006, we will spend about $320 billion on oil imports this year. Most of the world's oil is concentrated in places that are either hostile to American interests or vulnerable to political upheaval and terrorism. And demand for oil will increase far more rapidly than we expected just a few years ago. Within 25 years, the world will need 50 percent more energy than it does now.

With these basics in mind, my message is that the balance of realism has passed from those who argue on behalf of oil and a laissez faire energy policy that relies on market evolution, to those who recognize that in the absence of a major reorientation in the way we get our energy, life in America is going to be much more difficult in the coming decades. No one who cares about U.S. foreign policy, national security, and long-term economic growth can afford to ignore what is happening in Iran, Russia, Venezuela, or in the lobby of the Corinthia Hotel in Tripoli.

No one who is honestly assessing the decline of American leverage around the world due to our energy dependence can fail to see that energy is the albatross of U.S. national security.

We have entered a different energy era that requires a much different response than in past decades. What is needed is an urgent national campaign led by a succession of Presidents and Congresses who will ensure that American ingenuity and resources are fully committed to this problem.

We could take our time if this were merely a matter of accomplishing an industrial conversion to more cost effective technologies. Unfortunately, U.S. dependence on fossil fuels and their growing scarcity worldwide have already created conditions that are threatening our security and prosperity and undermining international stability. In the absence of revolutionary changes in energy policy, we are risking multiple disasters for our country that will constrain living standards, undermine our foreign policy goals, and leave us highly vulnerable to the machinations of rogue states.

The majority of oil and natural gas in the world is not controlled by those who respect market forces. Geology and politics have created petro-superpowers that nearly monopolize the world's oil supply. According to PFC Energy, foreign governments control up to 77 percent of the world's oil reserves through their national oil companies. These governments set prices through their investment and production decisions, and they have wide latitude to shut off the taps for political reasons.

I am not suggesting that markets won't eventually come into play to move America away from its oil dependence. Eventually, because of scarcity, terrorist attacks, market shocks, and foreign manipulation, the high price of oil will lead to enormous investment in and political support for alternatives. Given enough time, overcoming oil dependence and imbalances is well within the scope of human, and indeed American, ingenuity. The problem is that such investment cannot happen overnight, and even if it did, it will take years or even decades to build supporting infrastructure and change behavior. In other words, by the time a sustained energy crisis fully motivates the market, **we are likely to be well past the point where we can save ourselves.** Our motivation will come too late and the resulting investment will come too slowly to prevent the severe economic and security consequences of our oil dependence. **This is the very essence of a problem requiring government action.**

The first step is to admit how grave the problem is. Hopefully, we will look back on President Bush's declaration that America is "addicted to oil" as a seminal moment in American history, when a U.S president said something contrary to expectations and thereby stimulated change. **Like President Nixon using his anti-communist credentials to open up China** or President Johnson using his Southern roots to help pave the way for the Civil Rights Act, **President Bush's standing as an oil man would lend special power to his advocacy, if he chose to initiate an all-out campaign for renewable energy sources.**

Six Threats

As a national security problem, energy is unique in that the risks we face from this single condition are diverse and are intensifying simultaneously. In fact, our energy dependence creates at least six different threats that could directly or indirectly undermine American security and prosperity.

Each of these threats could be the subject of its own speech, but today, I will provide an abbreviated review.

First, as we have seen, oil supplies are vulnerable to natural disasters, wars, and terrorist attacks that can disrupt the lifeblood of the international economy. The entire nation felt the spike in prices caused by Hurricanes Katrina and Rita last year. But these shocks, which helped send the price of oil to $70 a barrel, were minor compared to what would occur if major oil processing facilities in Saudi Arabia were sabotaged. In late February, terrorists attempted such an attack. They penetrated the outer defenses of Saudi Arabia's largest oil processing facility with car bombs before being repulsed. A successful terrorist attack – either through conventional ground assaults, suicide attacks with hijacked aircraft, terrorist inspired internal sabotage, or other means – would be devastating to the world economy. Al-Qaeda and other terrorist organizations have openly declared their intent to attack oil facilities to inflict pain on Western economies.

Recently, we have also seen the shutdown of a fifth of Nigeria's production by militants, and Iraq's continuing struggle to expand its oil production capacity amidst terrorist attacks.

The vulnerability of oil supplies is not a new concern. But the lack of spare oil production capacity is new. As recently as four years ago, spare production capacity exceeded world oil consumption by about ten percent. As world demand for oil has rapidly increased in the last few years, spare capacity has declined to less than two percent. Thus, any major disruption of oil creates scarcity that will drive prices up.

These circumstances require massive expenditures to preserve our oil lifeline. One conservative estimate puts U.S. oil-dedicated military expenditures in the Middle East at $50 billion year.

Second, over time, even if oil and natural gas supplies are not disrupted in dramatic ways that produce local or global economic shocks, worldwide reserves are nevertheless diminishing. This is occurring within the context of explosive economic growth in China, India, Brazil, and many other nations. The demand for energy from these industrializing giants is creating unprecedented competition for oil and natural gas.

Americans paid 17 percent more for energy in 2005 than in the previous year. That increase accounted for 40 percent of the rise in the consumer price index. Last November, we spent more than $24 billion on oil imports, accounting for more than a third of our trade deficit.

To meet world oil demand, the International Energy Agency estimates a **need for $17 trillion in investment**, with the **bulk going to the Middle East**. But political and economic conditions may not let this investment happen. Even if some investment does occur and reserves prove to be much larger than anticipated, there is no guarantee that hostile governments will either choose to develop new capacity or make any new oil available to the United States.

In the decades to come, price will not be the only issue. We will face the prospect that the world's supply of oil may not be abundant and accessible enough to support continued economic growth in both the industrialized West and in large rapidly growing economies. **As we approach the point where the world's oil-hungry economies are competing for insufficient supplies of energy, oil will become an even stronger magnet for conflict and threats of military action, than it already is.**

Third, the use of energy as an overt weapon by producing nations is not a theoretical threat of the future; it is happening now. Oil and natural gas are the currency through which energy-rich countries leverage their interests against import dependent nations such as ours. Iran has repeatedly threatened to cut off oil exports to selected nations if economic sanctions are imposed against it.

Similarly Hugo Chavez in Venezuela has issued threats of an oil export embargo against the United States.

In January, Ukrainians were confronted by a Russian threat to cut off natural gas exports in mid-winter if Ukraine did not submit to a four-fold price increase. Russia took action to deny some natural gas to Ukraine. The dispute led to sharp drops in gas supplies reaching European countries that depend on natural gas moving through Ukrainian pipelines from Russia. Russia charged that Ukraine was diverting gas intended for Austria, Italy, France, Hungary and other European nations.

Eventually, the confrontation was resolved with a near doubling of the price of natural gas sold by Russia to Ukraine. In contrast, Russia did not inflict such a price increase on Belarus, considered by Moscow to be a good partner, compared to the pro-Western Ukrainian government. The episode underscored the vulnerability of consumer nations to their energy suppliers.

We are used to thinking in terms of conventional warfare between nations, but energy is becoming the weapon of choice for those who possess it. It may seem to be a less lethal weapon than military forces, but a natural gas shutdown to Ukraine in the middle of winter could cause death and economic loss on the scale of a military attack. Moreover, in such circumstances, nations would become desperate, increasing the chances of armed conflict and terrorism. The use of energy as a weapon might require NATO to review what alliance obligations would be in such cases.

Fourth, even when energy is not used overtly as a weapon, energy imbalances are allowing regimes in countries that are rich in oil and natural gas to avoid democratic reforms and insulate themselves from international pressure and the aspirations of their own people.

We are seeing Iran and Venezuela cultivate energy relationships with important nations that are in a position to block economic sanctions. For decades, we have watched Saudi Arabia and other Gulf states use oil wealth to create domestic conditions that prevent movement toward democracy. In Russia and Nigeria, energy assets have offered opportunities for corruption. In many oil rich nations, oil wealth has done little for the people, while ensuring less reform, less democracy, fewer free market activities, and more enrichment of elites.

Beyond the internal costs to these nations, we should recognize that we are transferring hundreds of billions of dollars each year to some of the least accountable regimes in the world.

Some are using this money to invest abroad in terrorism, instability, or demagogic appeals to populism.

At a time when the international community is attempting to persuade Iran to live up to its non-proliferation obligations, our economic leverage on that country has declined due to its burgeoning oil revenues. If one tracks the arc of Iran's behavior over the last decade, its suppression of dissent, its support for terrorists, and its conflict with the West have increased in conjunction with its oil revenues, which soared by 30 percent in 2005.

Sometimes observers comfort themselves with the thought that most U.S. imports come from friendly nations such as Canada and Mexico, rather than from Iran or other problematic countries. But oil is a globally priced commodity. Even if our dollars are not going directly to Iran, this does not mean that our staggering consumption of oil is not contributing to the price paid to Iran by other consumers.

Fifth, the threat of climate change has been made worse by inefficient and unclean use of nonrenewable energy. In the long run this could bring drought, famine, disease, and mass migration, all of which could lead to conflict and instability.

There are no unilateral solutions to climate change. I have urged the Bush Administration and my colleagues in Congress to return to a leadership role on the issue of climate change. I have advocated that the United States must be open to multi-lateral forums that attempt to achieve global solutions to the problem of greenhouse gases.

Our scientific understanding of climate change has advanced significantly. We have better computer models, more measurements and more evidence -- from the shrinking polar caps to expanding tropical disease zones for plants and humans -- that the problem is real and is caused by man-made emissions of greenhouse gases, including carbon dioxide from fossil fuels.

Sixth, our efforts to stem terrorist recruitment and prevent terrorist cells and training grounds in the developing world are being undercut by the high costs of energy. The economic impact of high oil prices is far more burdensome in developing countries than in the developed world. Generally, developing countries are more dependent on imported oil, their industries are more energy intensive, and they use energy less efficiently.

The United Nations Conference on Trade and Development estimates that non-OPEC developing nations spend 3.5 percent of their GDP or more on imported oil -- roughly twice the percentage paid in the main OECD countries. World Bank research shows that a sustained oil-price increase of $10 per barrel will reduce GDP by an average of 1.47 percent in countries with a per-capita income of less than $300. Some of these countries would lose as much as 4 percent of GDP. This compares to an average loss of less than one half of one percent of GDP in OECD countries. Some nations, such as Nepal and the Democratic Republic of the Congo, would experience GDP losses from a sustained $10 increase in the price of a barrel of oil that are twice the amount of foreign assistance that they receive from the United States. Even a nation like Ethiopia, which receives the substantial sum of $134 million in U.S. assistance because it is a focus country of the President's AIDs initiative, would see almost all of this offset by a $10 oil price increase.

Last week I chaired a Senate Foreign Relations Committee hearing on the nomination of Randy Tobias to be the new Administrator for USAID. In this capacity he would oversee a large share of our foreign assistance budget, which now exceeds $20 billion per year. This budget is intended to meet our humanitarian goals, but its success is also directly linked to national security.

But all of this effort and money, in essence, can be wiped out merely by an increase in the price of energy.

Without a diversification of energy supplies that emphasizes environmentally friendly energy sources that are abundant in most developing countries, the national incomes of energy poor nations will remain depressed, with negative consequences for stability, development, disease eradication, and terrorism.

Each of these six threats from energy dependence is becoming more acute as time passes. Any of them could be the source of catastrophe. Any realistic American foreign policy must redeploy diplomatic, military, scientific, and economic resources toward solving the energy problem.

The basic dilemma for U.S. energy policy is how can our government speed up the transition to alternative renewable energy sources so that we can prevent irreparable harm to our nation or the world associated with these threats? The realist must ask: how can we shape our energy future before it shapes us in disastrous ways?

Working Toward Energy Security

American energy policy to date has suffered from two fundamental flaws. First, we have let two decades of relatively cheap oil and natural gas deepen our dependence on imports. An approach that focuses on research, while ignoring deployment of new fuels will not meet our national security challenge.

The second flaw is that we have lacked a truly comprehensive energy policy with energy security as a strategic goal. American energy policy has been focused on a narrow definition of energy security that strived to ensure sufficient supplies at affordable prices. This has translated into policies promoting diversification in supplies of oil and natural gas, with little emphasis on energy alternatives. A policy that relies on a finite resource concentrated in a few countries is doomed to failure. Our long-term security and prosperity require sufficient, affordable, clean, reliable, and sustainable energy.

A first component of energy security is to ensure sufficient supplies. Our energy intensity per unit of GDP has steadily decreased, but our energy consumption is still projected to increase by more than a third over the next twenty-five years. This demand scenario is not inevitable. Public policy can do more to promote efficiency while still growing the economy. Expanded programs to enhance energy efficiency in appliances, building construction, and industry are all necessary to keep our energy intensity declining.

One third of our projected energy growth is in oil, a majority of which we have to import. I have co-sponsored a bipartisan bill with Senators Bayh and Lieberman that would require federal agencies to implement a plan to reduce U.S. oil consumption by 10 million barrels a day by 2031. The legislation contains many provisions to enhance energy conservation -- from tire efficiency to reduced school bus idling to light-weight materials research.

Automakers have a central role to play in improving our oil efficiency. We are working to close the SUV CAFE standards loophole, and to get more hybrids and flex-fuel vehicles on the road. A fleet of hybrid, and future plug-in hybrids, that run on E85 could reduce our oil use by 10 million barrels a day. The bill I have co-sponsored removes the cap on the number of tax rebates for hybrid vehicles. It also fosters demand by requiring that 30 percent of the government auto fleet be hybrids and advanced diesels. With increased demand for fuel efficient cars, new manufacturing facilities will be built that provide jobs for Americans.

In partnership with the American auto industry, we should provide a set of incentives that give them the opportunity to regain their strength and save jobs through innovation. This bill offers a 35 percent tax credit for automakers to retool their factories so that they can make fuel efficient, advanced technology vehicles.

Affordability of energy supplies also remains a key goal for energy security. Crude oil still hovers around $60 a barrel, and last October's price for natural gas was more than double what it had been in the previous year. These high energy prices increase inflation and inhibit future economic growth.

Elevated oil and natural gas prices do have the benefit of making alternative fuels more competitive. With the end of twenty years of low oil and gas prices, investment in alternative fuels has surged. **As more is invested, innovation in technology and production will drive prices down further. That is why it is so important to get the first cellulosic ethanol facilities up and running.**

The President said in his State of the Union address that he wanted to make cellulosic ethanol "practical and competitive within six years." In fact, one plant is ready to be built in Idaho, and many others could be built within the six-year time frame. I have asked the President to make sure that the loan guarantees that Congress authorized for cellulosic ethanol production are in place by this summer.

As alternative fuels become more competitive, oil and gas producers have strong incentive to drop prices to kill the competition. Investors need to know that alternative energy initiatives will continue to be competitive. A revenue-neutral $35 per barrel price floor on oil would provide the security investors need. At this price, alternative fuels like cellulosic ethanol, shale and tar sands oil, and Fischer-Tropsch diesel could still compete with regular gasoline.

Many analysts say that expensive oil is here to stay, but most energy investors are hesitant to take on that risk. A modest price floor for oil that we may never reach would provide a major stimulation for energy alternatives.

Long-term energy security also requires the use of clean energy, a third component of energy security. As long as we continue to consume fuels that do not burn cleanly or cannot have their damaging gases sequestered, we will continue to pay environmental costs and will remain vulnerable to a climate change induced disaster.

The Congress must pass legislation establishing a cap and trade mechanism. A cap and trade system would provide regulatory certainty, reward innovation to improve energy efficiency, and provide strong market incentives for clean renewable fuels. Any such system should give credit for carbon sequestration in coal-fired plants and allow farmers and foresters to sell credits for the carbon they sequester.

I have introduced a resolution that calls for America to lead other nations to new agreements under the United Nations Framework Convention on Climate Change. Thanks to new technology, we can control many greenhouse gases with proactive, pro-growth solutions, not just draconian limitations on economic activity. Industry and government alike recognize that progress on climate change can go hand in hand with progress on energy security, air pollution, and technology development.

Even as we strive to reduce the prevalence of fossil fuel in our energy portfolio, pragmatism requires that we diversify to the greatest extent possible our sources of oil and natural gas. I have supported opening ANWR for exploration. While we continue to debate production there and on the outer continental shelf, we have to carefully consider both the security and economic benefits of more exploration, as well as the environmental costs.

We must also ensure that we are not wasting fossil fuel resources in end-use that could be fueled by other means. I am encouraged by DuPont's commitment to replacing petrochemicals with bio alternatives. This wise business choice leaves DuPont less vulnerable to price spikes than competitors who still rely exclusively on oil and gas.

With natural gas prices high, there is now a shift to coal-fired electrical generation. New plants should favor coal, which we have in abundance, over natural gas. I continue to vigorously support the deployment of clean coal technology with carbon sequestration.

We can also use coal to reduce our oil dependence. The Energy Bill included legislation I coauthored with Senator Obama authorizing $85 million for federal research into the production of coal-based transportation fuels. One of the technologies that will be encouraged by this program, the Fischer-Tropsch process, yields a diesel fuel that is compatible with existing vehicle technology. It is superior to oil-derived fuel with respect to performance and emissions.

Another critical component of reliability is protection of the physical infrastructure and transit of our energy supplies. Terrorists have made clear their intentions to destroy refineries and pipelines worldwide. At home, in addition to power plants, ports, refineries, and platforms, we have 160,000 miles of oil pipelines. As the United States considers liquefied natural gas and nuclear facilities, we must be vigilant to the security implications.

While diversity in supplies at home and abroad is necessary for more reliable energy in the coming decades, diversification of sources for oil and gas is an outdated strategy that will never bring energy security. Reserves are too concentrated and infrastructure too vulnerable. Real diversity can only be achieved by an energy portfolio dominated by sustainable energy, the final component of energy security.

As we make policies to influence the composition of our future energy portfolio, we should strive to consume fewer hydrocarbons than we can produce domestically. This means more clean coal and renewable fuels of all types. I am encouraged that some states and municipalities are taking the initiative to increase their use of renewables. With Congressman Pete Visclosky, I am advocating a bill that will do that for Indiana.

Our policies should be targeted to replace hydrocarbons with carbohydrates. Obviously this is not a short-term proposition, but we can off-set a significant portion of demand for oil by giving American consumers a real choice of automotive fuel. We must end oil's near monopoly on the transportation sector, which accounts for 60 percent of American oil consumption.

I believe that biofuels, combined with hybrid and other technologies, can begin to move us away from our extreme dependence on oil in the next decade. Corn-based ethanol is already providing many Midwesterners with a lower-cost fuel option. Most of this is in a 10 percent ethanol mix, which is fully compatible with nearly all vehicles. I have recently called for my home state of Indiana to mandate that all gas stations in the state offer a 10 percent blend.

Cellulosic ethanol, which is made of more abundant and less expensive biomass, is poised for commercial take-off. I am pleased the President now supports the ethanol research that began under my legislation in 2000. I have long championed a renewable fuels standard, and we finally passed a 7.5 billion gallon ethanol mandate in the 2005 energy bill. The bill I am co-sponsoring with Senators Bayh and Lieberman will increase the proportion of ethanol from cellulose that will be in that mix.

As our domestic ethanol industry strengthens and demand grows, we will have to revisit the tariff we put on ethanol imports. We do not want to trade oil import dependency for biofuel import dependency, but trade in alternative energy also creates jobs, provides new markets for our advance technology, and diversifies our own supply. In the end, I believe the United States is well positioned to produce ethanol at competitive rates.

We have to make sure that consumers have access to E85 ethanol. Already there are millions of E85 capable vehicles on the road. I have introduced legislation that would require manufacturers to install flexible-fuel technology in all new cars in the next ten years. This is an easy and cheap modification, which allows vehicles to run on a mixture of 85 percent ethanol and 15 percent gasoline, and will make their products more attractive to consumers.

Next we have to make sure that consumers can buy the E85 fuel. I'm pleased that many independent gas station owners are taking advantage of the tax credit for E85 pump installation that we passed in the energy bill. I have co-sponsored legislation that would back loans for even more E85 pumps. The next challenge is to get E85 distributed through the big gas station chains. I've asked the oil majors about this, and they have said that sufficient demand for E85 does not exist. But demand will not develop for something that consumers do not have an option to buy. **It is time for the oil companies to make E85 available to the consumer. If these companies do not take advantage of the incentives Congress has provided, I would be in favor of legislation mandating that they install E85 pumps in appropriate markets.**

There is still more work to be done to tilt our energy balance toward alternative fuels. That is why Senator Obama and I will soon introduce a new bill that will promote other means to move these fuels into additional markets and make them more widely available for consumers. Among many provisions, the Obama-Lugar bill would create an alternative diesel standard comparable to the renewable fuels standard that I helped put into the 2005 energy bill. It would also provide new incentives for the production of flexible fuel vehicles. We believe that U.S. national security will be served by more robust coordination of all the elements that contribute to energy security. Consequently, the bill also would establish the post of Director of Energy Security, who would answer to the President.

Energy Partnerships

As we pursue energy security at home, we must seek energy partnerships abroad. This week, I will introduce framework legislation that calls for a realignment of our diplomatic priorities to meet energy security challenges. Partnerships with foreign governments can help speed our conversion to real energy security, rebalance power in geopolitics, and open new markets for fuel technologies.

The "Energy Diplomacy and Security Act" calls upon the Federal Government to expand international cooperation on energy issues. This bill will enhance international preparedness for major disruptions in oil supplies. A particular priority is to offer a formal coordination agreement with China and India as they develop strategic petroleum reserves. This will help draw them into the international system, providing supply reassurance, and thereby reducing potential for conflict.

The bill would also stimulate regional partnerships in the Western Hemisphere. Most of our oil and virtually all of our gas imports come from this Hemisphere. The bill creates a Western Hemisphere Energy Forum modeled on the APEC energy working group. This would provide a badly-needed mechanism for hemispheric energy cooperation and consultation.

Finally, the bill calls for international partnerships with both energy producers and consumers. In addition to seeking new avenues of cooperation, the bill is intended to give focus to existing bilateral energy dialogues, which have lacked clear objectives and political backing.

We must engage major oil and natural gas producers. We should advocate more transparency, improved investment climates, and greater infrastructure security. Oil exporting states wield power for which we must account. Not working with these states will lead to unproductive political showdowns and conflict. Even in challenging relationships such as Venezuela and Russia, we must explore how to improve our energy dialogue.

Strategic energy partnerships with other major consuming countries are crucial for our national security. Energy security is a priority we hold in common with other import dependent countries, which constitute 85 percent of the world's population. Strategic partnership for energy security with the world's largest consumers will increase leverage in relation to petro-states. In November, I introduced S. 1950, a bill that specifically targets India for enhanced cooperation on alternative energy sources, such as clean coal technology and biofuels.

To close, I would like to express my optimism for the future. Our current energy balance is the result of industrial and consumption choices of the past. Despite our import dependence today, the U.S. is in a strong position to choose a different path, a path toward real energy security. Success would free future generations of Americans from the energy dilemma that threatens to compromise our security and prosperity. It could also lead to opportunities in many new industries that could reinvigorate our economy. These are problems that can be solved. We must act now. We must act together.

Thank you.

# # #

CHAPTER 5

THE FEDERAL GOVERNMENT AND REAL ESTATE---GI & FHA

After world war II ended and the service men had come home, the Government decided to help the GI's buy a house. The Government established the Veterans Administration. As part of this act, was the GI bill which was to assist the Veteran to buy their first house. This was a just and appreciated asset to millions of Veterans.

This type of legislation proved to be a great asset to the economy. It stimulated home building, and all the supplies that went with it. Also, all the items that went into the finished house, such as appliances, furniture, flooring and a number of other household items. It helped the financial businesses who carried the mortgages for the new owners and guaranteed by the Government. With all this activity, the economy was booming.

This proved to be such a great plan, the Government decided to help the non-military Citizens in the lower income bracket who could not afford to buy a house. This plan was the Federal Housing Administration. This plan was similar to the GI plan. The major difference was a small down payment and a monthly fee to pay for the FHA Insurance Policy. This plan proved to be very popular and millions of people bought houses that could not have afforded to buy a house any other way, except maybe on Contract.

The problem I see with both plans currently is the large number of Government employees involved in the plans. I believe that both plans should be maintained by licensed and bonded Mortgage Companies. The Government could provide rules and regulations for the Mortgage Companies to follow. Penalties would be assessed against the mortgage companies for violations of the rules. In cases of default on the mortgage by the home owner, the house would be listed with a local Realty Company for sale at an appraised price. If the mortgage company looses money on the Mortgage, they will be allowed to deduct this loss on their Federal tax return.

Government bureaucracies are not always the best or the most frugal type to operate a business. The complication in obtaining the mortgage loan in the first place is bad enough, but it is nothing compared to selling a repossessed home. Talk about red tape.

All the unnecessary paper work required by the government, and the bidding process can be eliminated if the FHA bows out of the Real Estate market. Think of the millions that can be saved by letting the professional mortgage people do the work.

How many thousands of Government employees now are drawing a pay check, provided health insurance and a retirement package in order to operate the FHA and VA Real Estate Departments?

CHAPTER 6

TRANSPORTATION

Transportation is in need of drastic updating. The interstates are overcrowded, especially with semis. Road rage is on the rise and more and more accidents are caused by semis.

It is like Russian roulette driving the Interstates with all the semis and motor homes on the roads. If you are in the passing lane, you can't even see the road signs for the semis.

Many States are planning new highways, and adding lanes to eliminate the problem. This, my friend is not the solution. Building new highways and gobbling up thousands of acres of farm land, when we should be trying to conserve land, is not the answer. The problem isn't the space needed for more Interstates. It is the mode of transportation and the mindset of the Federal Government. The U. S. must endorse a high speed rail system that will take thousands of semis off our interstates. I said endorse, not operate. We have sufficient evidence that the Government does not know how to operate a railroad. Did you ever hear of Amtrak? This little adventure is costing taxpayers millions, no billions, to haul a few commuters to work. Federal contributions for fiscal year 2001 was $573 million, 2002 it was $1.1 billion, 2003 it was $1.0 billion, 2004 it was $1.2 billion, 2005 it was $1.2 billion. I strongly believe they should sell Amtrak to private interest or even give it away would be a bargain for the taxpayers.

We need a High Speed Rail System in this Country ASAP to eliminate so many semis on our highways, and to haul freight as well as passengers. The money spent on Amtrak should be spent on development of this form of transportation. I don't want the Government to own or operate this system, because it has been proven that private enterprise can and will do a better job. If they need a little help on magnetic levitation trains, they can get assistance from Japan. Japan operates the most efficient and convenient rail system in the world. This tightly scheduled, safe, quick and punctual rail service is provided by Japan Railways Group. Japan offers many levels of service from sleek high-speed "bullet trains" to their more humble country cousins and their crowded commuter counter parts.

The Bullet Train is the high speed trains that serve as the heart of Japan's rail transportation system. In almost 40 years since it opened, the Bullet Trains have carried over six billion passengers without a single serious accident. The Bullet Train can boast not only of its high speed, the fastest at 300 kilometers per hour, but also its frequency. For example, at least six trains per hour operate between Tokyo and Shin-Osaka Station during the daytime. Most foreign visitors arrive in Japan through either Narita Airport or Kansai Airport. Japan Rail Group offers the most convenient shuttle train service between the airports and downtown. It would be wise for the US Transportation Dept. head, to take a couple of Senators, and a few experienced Railroad Executives to Japan and make a thorough study of this great mode of transportation system. The right-of-way on the U. S. Interstates could be used for the HSRS.

It is way past time to do something about our overcrowded Interstates. Semis and motor homes are a safety problem. Most of the accidents are caused by semis. Do you think for one minute that the members of Congress are aware of the congestion on our highways today? If you answered affirmative, you have not been paying attention. To get Congress to address this serious problem, how about having some of their big time donors to their campaigns each election time donate the gasoline to make the trip from Washington to Miami on Interstate 95. You know on their measly salary they can't afford the gasoline required to make the trip. Of course Exxon Mobile would be delighted to chip in since they have so many friends in Washington. Exxon Mobile in the Third quarter of 05 only had a net income just shy of ten billion dollars. Would you like to place a bet that Congress would be ready to do something about our overcrowded highways after this trip? A few close calls with the semi crowd should do it.

New flash just in from the Office of Public Affairs. August 15, 2005

We finally have a man in Washington that is making sense and I congratulate him. He is the Secretary of Transportation, Norman Y. Mineta. Here is his statement concerning Amtrak reform, delivered at the U.S. Department of Transportation following the Senate Commerce committee hearing on Amtrak.

As you know, I have been traveling the nation in the past few months, talking to railroad workers and governors, community leaders, mayors, and commuters, to deliver the message that Amtrak cannot continue on its present course.

Today, happily, I am joined in this mission by Amtrak itself. After some 34 years and **$29 billion** of taxpayers' money, Amtrak is now acknowledging that its current business model is unsustainable and in need of serious reform.

I also welcome the news that the Senate Commerce, Science and Transportation Committee is prepared to work to pass legislation that helps avoid a financial collapse of Amtrak. But we need action this year to guarantee that intercity rail passengers and taxpayers have the service and accountability that they deserve.

Amtrak's strategic reform proposal adopts a number of the same principles in the Bush reform proposal that was delivered to Congress last week. But the important thing to note is that we have agreement in a number of areas and we all agree on saving intercity passenger rail.

President Bush's reform puts us on a new path that will bring solvency and new life into a dying railroad.

Skeptics of our plan like to say that there is no place in the world where passenger trains run at a profit. And I would like to seriously beg to differ.

I just returned from a trip to Asia where I saw firsthand how the Japanese have transformed failed passenger rail into a model of efficiency. For decades, Japan National Railway was a heavily subsidized train service that operated routes that nobody used and was known for its inefficient structure and poor financial service.

But in 1987, Japanese leaders had the courage to break up the railway into six smaller companies that are today known around the world for their on-time performance, cutting-edge technology, and high profit levels. So Japan has shown that there is a better way to run a railway, and I believe that we can also find a better way. I stand ready to work with the Congress to find that better way, and find it this year.

Bravo Mr. Secretary Mineta.

Just don't stop at passenger service. Think what an impact it would make to also have excellent high speed freight service. That would take thousands of Semis off the highways daily. This would save on building new Interstates. It would save on road construction and repair. It would save the trucking companies on diesel fuel and gasoline, tires and engine wear, plus it should save on insurance. Produce and mail could be delivered faster, and cheaper. It also would prevent a multitude of accidents between semis and cars and save many lives. If we don't go to HSRS we are going to be forced to build more or larger interstates. A railroad using the interstate right-of-ways should be considerably more economical that building a six lane interstate.

Big oil has completely ruined one of the best airlines in the U S. ATA never had an accident, was excellent to travel with, and now look at them. They caused pilots and many other good paying jobs to be lost while big oil swims in profits. They had to file bankruptcy. They are not alone in financial trouble. Many other airlines had to file for bankruptcy. Many more people are taking trips by air for the same reason that I do.

It is not safe driving the Interstates any more. Pay attention congress, and do something about the transportation problems. Don't leave it all up to Mr. Mineta.

We haven't seen a good transportation system since the Red Ball Express. A trucking outfit operated by American GI's in Europe during WWII. This group of tough soldiers delivered everything needed to fight a war under some of the most dangerous conditions.

Now this is PORK.

In H.R. bill SEC. 1114. HIGHWAY BRIDGE PROGRAM

$18,750,000 per fiscal year for the construction of a bridge joining the Island of Gravina to the community of Ketchikan in Alaska. There are currently only 50 residents living on this Island. If you ask me this is the whole hog. This type of legislation must be stopped.

Another good reason for term limits and the line item veto for the President.

For good reason, this bill was defeated.

HYDROGEN FUEL

As I have stated earlier in this book, the Government says we should have Hydrogen Cell cars within ten to 15 years. This my friends, depends on how fast Japan comes out with a hydrogen cell car. This technology has been around since Nov 1968. I know this as a fact. In November of 1968 I read in a magazine about a company called Environetics, Inc. The founder of the company was Don Rosen with headquarters at 1581 S. Broadway, Gardena, California 90247. The article stated that the company had an engine with a fuel cell that had no emission. They demonstrated the engine to a group of potential buyers in a closed room. The company also said they could fly a small airplane around the Earth without refueling. I wrote to Mr. Rosen and ask if I could buy stock in his company. I never received an answer, so I assumed he sold the rights to big oil. I still have a copy of the letter I mailed to Mr. Rosen. This Company is not the only one that has been developing hydrogen fuel. Ztex Corporation of Woburn, Ma., Founded in 1983, is a hydrogen reformer and fuel cell development and manufacturing company. If the Government could have seen the future like it is now, we wouldn't be in the situation we are in today. This first fuel cell in 1968 was only 38 years ago.

And now they are trying to make us believe it will be 2015 or later before we enjoy the benefits from this invention.

For the sake of this Earth and its inhabitants, please stop the pollution.

CHAPTER 7

DISASTERS

The worst disaster to hit the United States since 1905 was when a hurricane hit Galveston, Texas. Back in 1905 the technology to track a hurricane and measure its wind speed was not possible, so the populace of Galveston had no advanced warning of the severity of the storm about to hit them. The one called Katrina brewing in the Gulf of Mexico in late August 2005 was a category four hurricane, headed straight for New Orleans. The people in New Orleans were warned by the Hurricane Center and the News Media that this was a very dangerous storm that could cause major damage. The Mayor, Ray Nagin announced on TV that everyone in New Orleans should evacuate the city immediately. He had no clue or plan to evacuate all Citizens from New Orleans. He failed to take into account that thousands of citizens of New Orleans had no means of transportation, and very little money. He also failed to consider all the people in hospitals, nursing homes, assisted living, in wheel chairs and in private homes not able to communicate with Government Officials. This was a complete goof on the Mayors part and no apology is acceptable from him. The Governor of Louisiana, Kathleen Blanco never bothered to call the Mayor to see if every possible thing had been done to protect the citizens of New Orleans. The Mayor had at his disposal 400 school buses that could have been used to transport the people out of harms way.

It is very obvious that the State of Louisiana had no contingency plan to deal with any type of emergency. Both the Mayor and the Governor tried to put the blame for help on President Bush. If both of them would have handled the situation in a professional way, all the people in New Orleans would have been evacuated, and the situation would have been extremely better. As a last "H" hour decision, the Super dome was opened for the thousands of people who were able to walk to the dome for protection. Even in this scenario, no plans ahead of the storm had been made to shelter people in the dome.

Naturally, no planning ahead meant the dome was not equipped to handle thousands for any length of time with food and water.

None of the three states, Louisiana, Alabama, or Mississippi had any contingency plan in place for a devastating storm such as Katrina.

Instead of blaming the Federal Government, each one of the fifty states should have a contingency plan to deal with hurricanes, tornados, earthquakes, floods, fires, droughts, tidal waves, riots and such. They must be ready to evacuate to a safe place, and have leaders responsible for specific actions. Let's not overlook terrorist attacks. Yes, I said terrorist attacks. You and I both know that there are approximately 5000 Terrorist in this Country that came in illegally. That is such a hard thing to do, sometimes they even have to walk across the border. It is no wonder the Border States are so disgusted with the Immigration Department. Their problem is with the thousands of Mexicans coming across the border. The real problem is the Terrorist coming across, and they are just waiting for the right time to hit us in as many places at one time as possible.

You have heard the Government trying to justify the illegals being here for menial labor that no one in America wants to do. Would you call roofing a house, painting a house, driving semis and other good jobs menial? The only thing I see going on is another way to get votes. As I have suggested to Senator Lugar, if the illegal Mexican males want to be in the U.S. so bad, have them volunteer to serve in the army for four years and if they come out with a good record or want to stay in, the U. S. will grant them citizenship. The way this Illegal problem is shaping up, it looks like we are buying Mexico on Contract but will never get a deed.

Another good example of a disaster is Government backed flood insurance. It is ridiculous to allow people to build in a flood plain. The Government is shelling out millions yearly for houses destroyed by floods. This is not a one-time incident. The home owner rebuilds, and along comes another flood from the same river and the Government is in hock again. This was very apparent in New Orleans when the dike did not keep Lake Pontchartrain from overflowing and destroying thousands of homes.

Granted, home owners are required to pay flood insurance when they live in a flood plain. However, when a home is destroyed on a yearly basis by flood, an annual payment of flood insurance in no way covers the cost of replacing the house. This is where you and I come in Mr. & Mrs. Taxpayer. Yes the money comes out of the taxes you pay.

Does this sound familiar? Business Corporations pay into the Pension Benefit Guarantee Corporation a certain amount to cover retirement benefits for Employees in case the Business is not able financially to meet their obligation. Well guess what? When a business is on the rocks, so to speak, the Executives find a way to line their pockets with million dollar deals so they can retire. However they do not pay sufficient amounts to pay all that is due to retired Employees. You guessed it. You and I pay for their retired Employees retirement with our tax dollars. This is beginning to look like we taxpayers may be paying for the retirement of Employees of General Motors, Ford and Chrysler. I sincerely hope not but it doesn't look good. And don't forget all the Airline Employees that have been put out of a job because of Big Oil.

To keep disasters from happening we must have the best trained FBI with the best possible equipment and determination to keep the Terrorist in check. We must maintain the best trained Air force, Army, Navy, Marines, Coast Guard, National Guard and all ready at immediate call to duty or combat. It is imperative that we have surveillance by satellites. We must control our borders and know what foreigners are doing here.

This is the age of Terrorist and we are not facing an enemy like we have in the past. We must adjust our way of dealing with these radical extremist as they put no value on human life. If wiretapping is essential, and I believe it is, let's do it. I could care less what the extreme Liberals think. It is imperative that we stop an attack on this Country.

You have witnessed what happened in London and Spain. It is just a matter of time until they strike here. Only this time it will make the 9/11 tragedy look small in comparison.

It will not be a one incident attack. I believe they will hit us in four or five places at once, to cause the most confusion. Don't be surprised if it is biological, chemical or nuclear warfare.

In my opinion we must close all our nuclear plants immediately, because we cannot protect them adequately. One explosion of a nuclear reactor would result in thousands of fatalities immediately and thousands later by radiation. We must be ready with adequate protection from germ warfare. I believe the Terrorist are experimenting with Bird Flu and Mad Cow disease now, and who knows what else. Better keep a couple months of bottled water, food, blankets, flashlight and a cell phone on hand in a safe place.

LIBERAL MADE DISASTER:

The wire tapping controversy brought to the attention of the public by the Liberals is another example of aiding the enemy, and trying to discredit the President.

All they are doing is aiding the enemy who now will change their mode of communication. Don't they realize they are putting your family and friends in harms way? You had better be prepared to cover your rear when the Terrorist strike again in the U S. This is the most outrageous political ploy by the Democrats since Clinton was in Office. I propose you take your suggestion to Iraq and suggest this nonsense in front of our Troops. The Liberals are so Anti-American when they are not in power.

They will try anything to sway the American voters to vote for a Democrat in the next election. They apparently do not know when to shut up and act like a true American. This was so apparent at the funeral of Mrs. Martin Luther King when former President Carter used his time for the eulogy to bash Bush. I'm sure all decent American people who watched this on Television were outraged. I said all decent Americans. Not fanatics, or ACLU members.

The tax system is a disaster:

The sales tax is probably the fairest tax for States if it is not required for staples and medicine. People with modest income should not have to pay high taxes. A flat tax seems to have a lot of support for replacing the income tax of the U. S. This type of tax would do away with the complicated paperwork of filing of the current tax system. This would also save the taxpayer the fee for having a CPA do your taxes. With this new tax system the Government should have more time to monitor large Corporations to be sure they are not ripping off the Stock Holders. Corporations should be held accountable for their expenses and earnings on an annual basis. And they should be audited by the U. S. if any Stock Holder complains of wrong doing. Executives of Companies should get permission to sell their stock holdings from the Securities and Exchange Commission at least 30 days in advance of the sale. This should eliminate fraud and cooking of the books. This will eliminate Stock Holders from being left to hold the bag. In the past Management has unloaded their stock, because they had information that they were on the edge of Bankruptcy. Poor Martha Stewart had to serve time for her insider information.

What does that make Kenneth Lay and former CEO Jeffery Skilling, who unloaded their stock before the Company, Enron went belly up? As in the case of Conseco, no Officer of the Corporation should be allowed to borrow money from the Company without the approval of the of the Board of Directors, and <u>adequate collateral.</u>

FREE ENTERPRISE, OR PRICE FIXING?

You be the judge:

I believe in free enterprise, to a point. The one thing I do not believe in is the billions of dollars of income generated by a Company that is fixing prices to gain excess profits. Yes I'm talking about Exxon Mobile. For the year 2004 they had a net profit of one billion dollars. That was not enough. In the year 2005 their profit ballooned to thirty six plus billion. Now that is not what I call free enterprise. I call that price fixing. The Government keeps saying the economy is great. Well it is not great for the consumer. Everything you buy is affected by the high fuel prices. Thousands of people have lost their jobs in the Airlines because of high gasoline prices. Thousands more are losing their jobs in the American Auto Industries because they do not have the energy efficient cars. The American Auto Industry went to sleep on new technology and did mot take advantage of new engines that run on batteries and gas. They were still able to sell their product. Now it is catching up time. A group of five inventors tried to sell Hybrid Engines to Ford, GM, and Chrysler about the year 2000 and they all declined. The Hybrid cars from Japan are taking over the market. The only way the Big Three will be able to regain any share of the market will be to introduce a competitive Hydrogen Car. Big Oil is going to keep ripping us off as long as the Government lets them do it.

This I want you to understand. Big Oil and the Automobile Companies along with the help of Congress have created this scenario. The Auto Companies were happy as long as the American consumers bought their cars and they kept congress happy. Of course Big Oil was happy as long as the Auto Companies and Congress both kept them happy. Never mind the new inventions coming out of Japan. People won't buy Japanese cars because of Pearl Harbor. Well all three overlooked one little incident. Most of the younger generation of America does not know anything about Japan bombing Pearl Harbor back on December 7, 1941. Most of the WWII Veterans are gone and most schools don't bother to teach history in schools anymore. That's one of the reasons why Americans are buying Japanese cars. They save money on gasoline, are very reliable and people want a dependable mode of transportation.

Now here is the BIG SHOCKER:

TRADE DEFICIT:

Buy gold and silver and put a stop loss order on your stocks or you will end up with nothing. The trade deficit is in excess of $725 Billion. The U.S. has a deficit in excess of $200 billion with China. They in turn put a lot of money into stocks, bonds, and other assets. If they decided to sell a tremendous amount of these assets, the stock market could tumble, the dollar would lose its value and this would make 1929 crash look like a picnic. Japan also has a lot of assets invested in the U. S. The Government had better figure out a way to change this trend or we are heading for a giant catastrophe.

DISASTER IN THE MAKING; ARE WE GIVING AMERICA AWAY?

Education in the USA has fallen to a new low. We have zero people with the ability to build bridges, operate a toll road, supervise operations at U. S. Ports, and operate parking lots at U. S. Airports. Perhaps if the Government did more for the schools, we could graduate young people intelligent enough to do these complicated duties that we have to hire foreign entities to do. By the way congress, when was the last time you had to be in session all day in a building with no air condition and in 90 degree heat? I would bet that a recess would be called immediately until the A/C was repaired. I have heard some very bad reports of the bad language and drugs going on in our schools. Children playing hooky and engaging in sex is rampant. As you no doubt have heard on TV about teachers having sex with students. The problem with the schools is partially the lack of great Teachers. They cannot keep the students interest in class. The studies are not interesting. This, my friends in Washington, needs a lot of attention.

What in the world is going on in Washington D. C.? Do we know where the money will go that we pay a United Arab Emirates to operate our Ports? For all we know they are funding Terrorist. Maybe they have heard of Freud and decided to use a little psychology on us to clear any doubt in our mind that they are our friends. Since we do not want to upset the United Arab Emirates I suggest that congress should pass a law that prevents the Government from leasing, contracting, or selling any U. S. property to a Foreign Country or Person. As for all the Foreign Countries currently with a lease agreement or contract, their agreements will **not** be renewed. The Japanese currently own

71

many parcels of Real Estate in Hawaii. Much of our farm land is owned my foreign entities. I believe this sets a very dangerous situation. I would hope congress would put a stop to this practice. Just remember that Saudi Arabia is supposed to be our friends, but eleven out of the twelve that hijacked the two American Airline Planes to destroy the Towers at the world Trade Center in New York City were from Saudi Arabia. They also are not helping us with oil prices. Any time oil goes down in price, OPEC of which Saudi Arabia is a member, reduces production until the price goes back up.

FAMOUS CLINTON QUOTE: INADVERTENTLY

As stated in a report by Chairman Issa of the Committee on Government Reform as of March 1, 2006.

Serious concerns have arisen regarding the implementation of the federal government's natural gas royalty payment program. Recent news is that the government may be unable to collect anywhere from $7 billion to $28 billion in natural gas royalties from leases of federal land and waters. This is particularly troublesome at a time when natural gas companies are continuing to post record earnings. There are several areas of concern.

One issue is whether some gas companies have failed to fulfill their contractual obligations to make royalty payments to the Department of the Interior. There is also a question whether the US government may have been underpaid in excess of $700 Million worth of royalties in 2005 on this basis alone.

Additionally, there is concern that the U.S. could be excluded from billions of royalties as a result of how the Deep Water Royalty Relief Act has been implemented. The Act was enacted to provide an incentive to gas companies to explore and extract oil and natural gas from U.S. waters. This could be accomplished by allowing the Secretary of the Interior and oil and gas companies, between 1996 and 2000, to enter into leases with a defined volume suspension and price threshold so that companies would be able to recover their capital investment before having to pay royalties on their profits. This came at a time when oil and gas prices were low and the interest in deep water drilling was lacking.

However, during 1998 and 1999, price thresholds were inexplicably not included as terms of the leases. As these wells are now beginning to reap billions in profits at a time of high gas prices, the effects of the lease terms are coming to fruition. As a result, the US may be unable to receive royalties from billions in gross revenues stemming from leases signed in 1998 and 1999.

The threshold provision " **was inadvertently dropped**" from more than 1,100 leases issued in 1998 and 1999, allowing the companies to avoid royalty payments, Walter Cruickshank, deputy director of the Mineral Management Service, said at this meeting.

This action in regards to the oil and gas leases took place in 1995 during the term of President William Jefferson Clinton.

LEASING THE MILITARY:

When are we going to lease out our Military? From the looks of things, we already are. However we are not getting paid. Instead we are paying to render a great service. It's not just the monetary, but the loss of precious lives. We have Military scattered all around the World. We have Military in Iraq, Pakistan, Germany, Kuwait, South Korea, Hawaii, and many other places around the Globe. Do we get paid for this service? Mostly we pay them the equivalent to a lease agreement. Most of the time we receive no merci beaucoup, gracious, or danke. Great Britain and Israel are the only countries that appreciate our effort to help them. The French Government does not show any respect for the sacrifice made by the American Military in WW II for freeing them from Mad Man Hitler. I do not believe this is the feeling of the French people. I was in WW II and I was in France. I saw only gratitude and relief for the freedom that was returned to them.

CHAPTER 8

DEMOCRATS ON LOCO WEED

The Democrats must be eating their salad with loco weed in it because they sure are going nuts as witnessed in Al Gores speech in Saudi Arabia. I cannot believe the anti President rhetoric that the likes of former Presidents and Vise President, Jimmy Carter, Wm. Clinton, Al Gore are spewing out and giving the enemy fuel to wage hate against us more so than they already are. Al Gore inciting the Muslins in Foreign Countries to hate us more than they do already. It looks like he is trying to start a revolt with the American Muslins. If he thinks this is going to enhance his ability to be nominated for President in the next election, he's badly mistaken. He couldn't even win his home State of Tennessee in his last try for President. I think what these three should do is go to Iraq and make one of those ridiculous speeches in front of a group of American Soldiers. If any of the three had any sons or daughters in the Military in Iraq, they would keep their mouths shut, but good. The liberals are not satisfied with exposing the wire tapping so the enemy could change their way of communicating. Now Gore says the U.S. is treating the Muslins bad here? I suppose we will behead them next. Did you get your idea for the speech from your ole buddy Bill Clinton? You don't stand a snow ball chance in, you no where, against Hillary in the nomination. She is a much greater Bull Slinger than you are. I apologize for leaving out Ted Kennedy and Jane Fonda but I am going to include them in my invitation. What invitation you ask? Well I thought a little trip with Vise President Cheney to Texas for a quail hunting trip would be nice.

I apologize to most Democrats. Some of my best friends are Democrats. It is the extreme far left Democrats that should not be classified as Democrats. A more suitable name for them would be Liberalcrats. I think the likes of Bill Arkin and a few others would be Fanaticrats.

Senator John Kerry destroyed his political life with one speech. Quote, "If you shirk your education, you could find yourself in the military, and spend some time in Iraq."

Some Politicians are so anxious to achieve a goal they will open their mouth before the brain has control once the words are spoken, no matter how hard they try they cannot undo what was said, the Public just won't buy. Is the War in Iraq our biggest problem? I say it is a toss up between the War with the Terrorist and the Illegals in this Country. The Illegals are fighting a war with the U.S. and it looks to me like they are winning. Both are big problems for the Government. President Bush is bound and determined to give the Illegals amnesty, in one form or another. The present Politicians are a bunch of wimps. Neither party has the courage to enforce the laws of this Government. We are being taken over by poor and needy people from Mexico. In the process we are being overrun with drug dealers, thieves, and criminals let go by the Mexican Authorities. Our schools are being overrun with Illegal Mexican Students. The Illegals will work for lower wages until they have forced the American people out of a job and then they will be demanding higher pay. The Government will be paying Unemployment Compensation to the Americans who have lost their jobs to the Illegals. The Judges in this Country have proved that they have no will to enforce the laws of this Country when an Illegal has been charged with a crime.

The hands of the Police are tied when they could be enforcing the laws of this Country.

If you don't help me make some drastic changes, we are headed for the downfall of the greatest Nation in the World.

CHAPTER 9

PREAMBLE TO THE CONSTITUTION

Before the U S Senate and the House of Representatives of the U S congress decide on any act of amnesty for the estimated twenty million illegal immigrants in this U.S.A.

I suggest they read the preamble of the constitution, until they understand it.

Preamble

We the People of the United States, in order to form a more perfect Union, establish Justice, insure domestic Tranquility, provide for the common Defense, promote the general Welfare, and secure the Blessings of Liberty to ourselves and our Posterity, do ordain and establish this Constitution for the United States of America.

1. MORE PERFECT UNION: This is not the case when the Government allows the laws of the U.S. violated by millions of Illegals to enter this Country and stage protest marches. This does not a more perfect Union make, and violates all aspects of the Preamble to the Constitution.

2. To insure domestic Tranquility means free from agitation of mind or spirit, and free from disturbance or turmoil. Illegals demanding citizenship, are causing all kinds of trouble.

3. Provide for the common defense. It has been proven over the past ten years plus that the U.S. cannot control the borders in the North or the South.

4. We have ample problems trying to protect the general welfare of thousands of U. S. Citizens who are homeless, under fed, in need of medical attention and many other social problems. We do not need twenty million more people to take care of, who have many of these same problems. It is the responsibility

of the Government from where they came, Mr. President of Mexico.

5. Secure the blessings of Liberty to Ourselves and our posterity. I am not over confident that we the Citizens of this great Country will be leaving the blessing of liberty to ourselves and our decedents after us. Congress, it is past time for you to address this problem and do the will of the majority of the people and not for your own self interest.

CHAPTER 10

THE IMAGINARY IMMIGRATION DEPARTMENT

The title of this chapter says it all. We have no control over Illegals coming into this Country.

Is this because the Immigration Department is a division of the Home Land Security Department? Does this make you feel safe? If this is any indication of the way HLSD is taking care of protecting the Citizens of America; we are in for a lot of trouble. How many Terrorist and drug dealers have entered the U.S. because of our open borders? Not just from Mexico but form Canada and we don't know from where else. It is estimated that we have five thousand terrorist in the U.S. because of our open borders? How do we stop this ridiculous situation? Read on and you will see how simple it is even though the Government of the U.S. seems to believe the only solution is amnesty. This is 2007 and the information I hear on the news is that President Bush is calling for a form of amnesty. Is this because the new President of Mexico would like it this way? This sure would help the economy of Mexico. I cannot believe what is going on in this Country.

We have tried to help Mexico with the National Free Trade Agreement. Apparently it is not helping the working class or they would not be coming to America trying to have a decent living. Part of the NAFTA would allow Mexican trucks to drive anywhere in the U.S. Currently they stop at the border and reload onto American trucks. We cannot allow this part of the agreement to be approved. This will be an invitation for more illegals and drugs to enter this Country. Our highways are already overcrowded with trucks and we certainly do not need anymore. I would be amazed if the Mexican trucks could pass and meet American safety standards. If I was in charge of Home Land Security I would disapprove of this arrangement feverishly. If the President wants to control the border, this plan should never be approved.

Now my friends it is time to help Bill O'Reilly by contacting your Senators and Representatives in Washington to put a stop to this. In my opinion instead off the President of Mexico complaining about the U.S. insensitivity to all the Mexican illegals coming to the U.S. to work and earn money to send back to Mexico, perhaps it is time he did something for his people so they don't have to be illegals to earn a decent living. I was under the assumption that NAFTA was supposed to help Mexico as well as the U.S. Instead of NAFTA helping the U.S. as promised it has caused a loss of jobs in the U.S. and the products made in Mexico do not always come up to the quality standards we counted on when the items were made in the U.S. MR Fox, you cannot have an economy by depending entirely on illegals sending money back to Mexico and tourism. You have a beautiful Country, you have jobs for the workers, so why not pay them a decent wage so they don't have to risk their lives and be away from their families in order to have a decent life. It is past time for you to take the initiative. Offer incentives for your people to stay in Mexico. If you cannot see what you are doing is wrong, you are heading down the wrong road. Rid your Government of greed.

Perhaps we could get Mr. Fox to come across the border and throw in his hat to run for President. It shouldn't be any trouble for him to cross the border. We have several million of his former citizens living in the U.S. at the present time. Since we allow all these Illegals to come across the border with no trouble at all, we surely can make an exception for him not being a legally born American citizen to run for President. Now if his illegal Mother would have been in the U.S. when he was born, he would be a legally born American citizen. This is another example of what is wrong with America. The truth is the Immigration Dept. is doing nothing to stop illegals from crossing our border. But how many could be Terrorist? Terrorist have been discovered in Canada and the Police have arrested several in the process of kidnapping the Prime Minister. If they are in Canada, you know we have them also. As a matter of fact, it is estimated that five thousand are here in the U.S.

The big theory why we need the illegals here is because they will do jobs that Americans will not do. The truth is the illegals will do the jobs for less pay.

The Government won't tell the truth. Many illegals are doing jobs for less pay, forcing Americans to go on welfare.

Did you know a group of citizens in Arizona, calling themselves Minute Men, are patrolling the border between Mexico and Arizona? They are protecting their borders because no one else will. Can you blame them? The Emigration Dept. sure isn't doing anything about the situation. I think we could save a lot of taxpayers money if we did away with the Emigration Dept.

Finally with the constant badgering of Bill O'Reilly of Fox News, the President of the U.S. is making a move to secure our border between the U.S. and Mexico. It is only eight years and twenty million Illegals too late. Remember one person can make a difference, and Mr. Bill O'Reilly of Fox New is making a lot of people wake up.

THE ILLEGALS ARE EXPRESSING THEIR UNLAWFUL RIGHT TO BE LEGAL:

The Illegals have taken over the Alamo again, so to speak, as it was witnessed on TV. Thousands took to the streets in major cities from California to Washington D.C. They were protesting because the U.S. Government was considering a bill to make Illegals guilty of a felony. They are showing their true colors by demonstrating in a Country where they have no right to be in the first place. If they think this is aiding their cause, they are badly mistaking.

They are not only agitating all American citizens, but they are causing the Mexican American citizens who came here legally to be upset. Even school children were blocking Interstate Highways and city streets. I wonder what teacher suggested this behavior. If they tried this in Mexico they would be tossed into jail. If they think this type of behavior will get them amnesty, they are wrong. Any politician who suggests amnesty will not be elected in the next term. Our government had better come up with a better plan to close our borders fast. This absolutely has to be stopped. Let's assume for a moment what would happen if this scenario was reversed. Let's assume that twenty million Illegal Americans were in Mexico. They protest in the streets, interrupt traffic, waving the American flag, because Mexico is going to charge them with a felony. Here is what would happen. The Mexican Army, if they still have enough men left to have an army, would load all the protesters in trucks and trains and take them to the U.S. border and turn them over to the American authorities.

If the Mexican Illegals want a country like the U.S. the twenty million here could all go back to Mexico and vote for who ever they wanted for President. Twenty million votes should swing the election their way. If they work at it they could have a great democracy also. If the Illegals refuse to go back to Mexico on their own, it is up to the U.S. to deport them. No if, ands or buts about it, they have to go until they learn that we the Citizens of this great nation will not tolerate Illegals being here. I am and I hope you are also putting all Politicians on notice that vote for any kind of amnesty for the Illegals, they will not be elected again.

PRESIDENT OF MEXICO:

Mr. President, it seems that your plan is working. Most of your Citizens have fled your country to be free. However, they will not be sending money back to Mexico. They want a decent life. They are fed up with your Government that caters to a favored few. This is not what democracy is all about. It seems that you and your peers think that you can get away with hoarding all the wealth. This only works for a period of time until the masses determine they have no say in the government. I'm sure it was fun while it lasted. Now it is time to face the consequences. Cuba and Castro would have faced the same fate if it wasn't for the Atlantic Ocean. Many Cubans have tried to flee Cuba on small boats and anything that would float. They risked their lives trying to reach the U.S.A. Some even perished in the attempt, that's how bad they wanted freedom. Iran, North Korea, Venezuela and a few other rogue countries will wise up after it is too late. People are not willing to be treated like animals. They deserve to be treated like humans, and have freedom. All the World deserves to have freedom and the sooner you Dictators realize this, the better your countries will be.

On this day 4/10/06, thousands of illegals demonstrated in the streets of most major cities of the U.S. demanding citizenship. I understand why they want to live here, and I think that is a great compliment to America. But there is a legal way and illegal way to become an American citizen. If they are here illegally, they have chosen the wrong way.

MY PLAN TO STOP ILLEGALS:

The Politicians are reluctant to recommend any plan to solve the Illegal Immigration problem. They know what needs to be done but for fear of losing their seat in Congress, they only make excuses.

I have a plan that will not even be necessary to build a fence across the border. The first item is to pass the amendment recommended by the Representative from Texas, the Hon. Ron Paul and Hon. Mr. Alexander. Amendment XIV Section 1. Simply states that any baby born on U.S. soil is automatically a citizen of the U.S.A. I agree with the proposal to put a stop to this ridiculous law. See Appendix Hon. Ron Paul of Texas. (See page 94 and 95, Amendment XIV Sect 1)

The second item to be implemented immediately is to make it a felony to hire any Illegal. The law should require a fine of $1000.00 dollars on the person or business for each Illegal hired. If convicted a second time, the fine will be $5000.00 for each Illegal and a jail sentence of one to five years in prison. It shall be required to furnish proof of Citizenship in order to obtain a drivers license or social security card. In addition, the law should state that it is unlawful to sell, lease, or rent housing of any kind to a person without proper identification.

In addition, a person with a green card or visa will not be allowed to own Real Estate in the U.S. until they obtain legal residency.

It is past time for the Government to enact a plan to stop this ploy for votes.

Comments on Immigration by Theodore Roosevelt

Theodore Roosevelt on Immigrants and being an AMERICAN

"In the first place we should insist that if the immigrant who comes here in good faith becomes an American and assimilates himself to us, he shall be treated on an exact equality with everyone else, for it is an outrage to discriminate against any such man because of creed, or birthplace, or origin. But this is predicated upon the man's becoming in very fact an American, and nothing but an American...There can be no divided allegiance here. Any man who says he is an American, but something else also, isn't an American at all. We have room for but one flag, the American flag, and this excludes the red flag, which symbolizes all wars against liberty and civilization, just as much as it excludes any foreign flag of a nation to which we are hostile...We have room for but one language here, and that is the English language...and we have room for but one sole loyalty and that is a loyalty to the American people."

Theodore Roosevelt 1907

CHAPTER 11

TAXES UPON TAXES
CAPITAL GAINS TAX

This tax should be abolished immediately. It has been proven that without this tax, more revenue is generated without it than with it.

EXAMPLE:

A person buys a rundown house, or HUD Repro, and we all know that there are plenty of these on the market. Why are there so many repossessions on the market? That is an easy one to answer. High risk buyers are allowed to buy a Government backed loan with no down payment and very little closing cost. After a year or two when the taxes, insurance, are added in, their monthly mortgage payment makes then unable to make their payment and they default on the loan. As I have said ever since I have been a REALTOR, the Government should not be in Real Estate.

They have thousands of people in HUD and VA housing. I do not know the amount of their budget, but it must be in the billions. I do not disagree to helping the Veterans and the underprivileged to buy a house, what I do disagree with is all the bureaucracy that is involved in buying a house and trying to sell a repossessed house from bankruptcy. I think Mortgage Companies should be giving an incentive to do the same type mortgages that the Government is doing except all the Government will do is back the Mortgage Companies. THE REALTORS WILL LOVE THIS NEW PLAN. No more complicated paper work to deal with. Repossessed houses will sell quicker, and the Buyer can do business with the Mortgage Company of their choice.

Now back to the Capital Gains Tax.

More revenue will be generated with all the material purchased to put the house in condition to put it on the market for resell. In addition the new owner will pay income taxes on the property when it is sold. Under the present property tax in Indiana, which should be abolished, the new assessed value will generate more taxes for Indiana. I will also add that the Indiana property tax is totally unfair. Why is it unfair you ask? The value for assessing the house for tax purposes is done by the County Assessor in the County where the property is located. The price is set based on similar houses that have sold in the area. Of course if no houses have been sold in the area, this makes it more of a problem for the Assessor who then uses his opinion. If three Assessors put a value on the same property, you would have three different prices. Not a very good example of establishing a true value. Both the Capital gains tax and the Indiana property tax should be abolished.

ESTATE TAX

This is absolutely the most outrageous tax that Congress has ever come up with.

Take for example a Farmer. A Farmer works himself to death for forty or fifty years, growing your food under all kinds of weather conditions. Sometimes he has a bumper crop and sometimes because of bad weather conditions he has a very poor crop. When he has a very poor crop, he may even loose money. If he is in to raising farm animals to sell, he has to depend on the market price. As we all know the market price fluctuates on several factors. Currently they are faced with high energy prices. Of course they do not depend on energy cost like the grain Farmer does. Now do you appreciate what a Farmer goes through? It is no picnic. I guess that is why the Farmer gets subsidy payments for different things. Some of which I am against. A good example is the peanut subsidy which was implemented back in 1932. That was because they needed help after the finical collapse of 1929. Do you believe it is still needed? I thought you would say no. Another great example of subsidies is the one they gave to Tobacco Farmers. After suing the Tobacco companies, they gave tobacco farmers a subsidy for not raising tobacco.

If the Farmer wants to pass the farm on to his heirs upon his death, the heirs have to pay an Estate tax. The heirs will be paying taxes on the farm when they take over, so why should they pay an Estate Tax? This is next to robbery and a sure fire way to discourage young people from being a farmer.

SOCIAL SECURITY TAX

The social security act was passed in 1935. It has had many amendments since that time. Is it now time to consider some improvements to keep it solvent? I think SS is a great plan for all Americans. There is no way that millions of Americans could live the lifestyle they currently have without SS. In order to live a little better and enjoy retirement, many Americans take part time jobs to supplement their income.

This way they can take vacations, play golf or whatever they enjoy.

In 1983 many amendments were made to SS. As the changes cover three full pages I am not going to show all the changes here, but you can read all of them on SS Amendments of 1983 signed 4/20/1983. I am only going to show two parts of the amendments. Part 1: Covers under Social Security the following groups: (1) General employees hired on or after January 1, 1984. (2) Current employees of the legislative branch not participating in the Civil Service Retirement System on December 31, 1983; and (3) all the Members of Congress, the President and the Vice-President, Federal Judges, and other executive-level political appointees of the Federal Government, effective January 1, 1984. Some modifications have been made since this amendment was approved. (See P.L. 98-118 and P-L- 98-369 for a modification. Also see P.L. 98-168 for a related provision.)

Originally SS was not to be taxed. However beginning in 1984, up to one-half of Social Security benefits as taxable income for taxpayers whose adjusted gross income, combined with half their benefits and any tax exempt interest they may have exceeds $25,000 for a single taxpayer and $32,000 for married taxpayers filing jointly. Benefits received by married taxpayers filing separately are taxable without regard to other income. Appropriate amounts equal to estimated tax liability to the SS trust funds.

In the beginning the social security tax was not to be taxed as income. The eligible had already been taxed on the money that was set aside for the day that they reached sixty five. In order to eliminate all this taxing, I believe it is past time to convince Congress that we are tired of PORK and need a cork in it. Is it time for another Boston Tea Party? Maybe a Washington Potomac swim party with lead bathing suits would be in order. I think Congress should enact a bill that violates the members from adding any pork to any bill. What say you? Would a LINE ITEM VETO ELIMINATE PORK? What say we try it?

CHAPTER 12

THE SOCIAL SECURITY ACT OF 1935 AND CONGRESS

Seventy years ago during the term of President Roosevelt the Social Security Act became law. Like any major undertaking it was controversial, but it has proved beneficial to many citizens in the U S A. Like any plan, it has its faults, mostly due to Congress. There is no way most retired people could live the lifestyle they enjoy without the benefit of Social Security.

After seventy years is it time to nix it or fix it? My opinion is that it needs to be tweaked a bit. Most good ideas can be improved over time from experience in use and President Bush thinks it is high time to explore some changes--. Only Congress has the power to make amendments to Social Security Act. As a matter of record, Congress didn't think the plan was good enough for them, so they decided to implement their own retirement plan. Their plan would make the goose that lay the golden egg green with envy. It makes my face red with anger. Not only is it taking advantage of their authority, it is offensive, greedy, and disgusting because of the way it is funded. The fund to supplement this nest egg comes from the General Fund and cost them nothing. The general fund is generated from your tax dollars. This is double dipping from the Social Security fund as well as the general fund. It is part of a retirement plan for Congress called a thrift plan. They pay a percentage into the plan which is matched by your tax dollars. Is it any wonder they hold on to that job as long as they can? If we the people demanded that Congress funded their own retirement plan with their own money, and had to retire on Social Security, how long do you think it would take for the Congress to cooperate with the President for a plan to improve Social Security?

Social Security has been the favorite propaganda tool used by the Democrat Party in the Presidential election each year beginning with the year that Republican Barry Goldwater from Arizona was running for the Office. It had the elderly people so convinced that they would lose their Social Security if Mr. Goldwater was elected, that it caused him to lose the election. Since this out and out lie was so successful, the Democrats have used one form or the other of it in every election since.

If Immigration was controlled, and all the twenty million illegals deported, Social Security would be solvent for many more years than forecast. It is so obvious that they would be drawing out more that they put in. This is not fair to the natural born American Citizen who has paid into the system all their working life.

You have heard of the Green Card proposal that President Bush is pursuing for the illegals. To me that just looks like an amnesty program to let the illegals stay here and become citizens of the U S. We cannot allow these illegals come into the U S and not be sent back where they came from until they can come back legally. This Green Card system is just an incentive to encourage more illegals to come across the border.

CHAPTER 13

ARE YOU GETTING THE MESSAGE YET?

The U.S.A. is at one of the most critical stages in our history. We are fighting the terrorist that consists of fanatics from Iraq, Iran, Syria, Afghanistan, Pakistan and Muslins from around the World. Throw in North Korea and Venezuela and that takes care of most of our enemies that want to destroy us. They fight to kill and make no distinction between women and children. They want to destroy anyone who is not a Muslim. They hate America, Great Britain and Israel, and anyone that does not believe in Allah.

With the threat of nuclear weapons in the possession of insane leaders such as North Korea and Iran, the possibility of destroying the Earth is a very real probability.

These idiots will stop at nothing. What they expect to gain by all these murders is a mystery to me. If they would wise up and realize what effort they are squandering on hate is destroying the World. Think what a glorious place Earth would be, if the same effort was directed to love of your fellow man.

The terrorist have proven time after time that they place no value on human life. The destruction of the World Trade Center proved this. Of course, when the accidental killing of terrorist women and children, all kinds of verbal rhetoric is voiced against the Americans, English and Jews.

In my opinion if the terrorist want to fight dirty, then I think we should show them what dirty is. Remember the static the U. S. received about abusing the prisoners at Guantanamo Bay? At least I don't recall a single one having their head chopped off.

What really irked me was the Americans Citizens complaining. As a matter of fact, we have had entirely too much criticism about fighting in Iraq. The far left media is an excellent example of a group of left wingers that still do not believe that we are at war with the terrorist. Some of our past presidents and Government Officials are not helping our war with the terrorist. Jimmy Carter had no clue of what to do when Iran was holding American citizens prisoner when he was president and he has no solutions for the present situation. Ronald Reagan became President when Jimmy Carters term ended. The first thing he did as President was to give Iran an ultimatum to release the American citizens or face the consequences. The American citizens were released immediately. As for past President Clinton while he was in office, he did nothing to stop terrorist attacks. I have already viewed my opinion of him in this book. Some of our current politicians still in power, such as Kennedy, Kerry, Hillary and a host of other Democrats are hurting our cause and putting our troops in harms way by encouraging the enemy with their speeches against President Bush. The New York Times is pressing the first amendment to the brink. All these people are doing is giving hope to our enemies.

The terrorist are sneaky and cowardly. They hide weapons, rocket launchers and bombs in private homes, churches, hospitals and centers of civilian population because they know the Americans, British, and Israelis will not fire on civilians. The coward Ben Laden may be a hero to his followers, but he is just a worthless piece of work who lets his worshipers blow themselves up.

Iran and North Korea are leading the way to destroy Civilization as we know it. Once they use a nuclear bomb that will be the beginning of the end of the World as we know it.

If the terrorist should win the war with nukes, they will loose the war to gain the world.

As we all know, Russia and China both have Atomic Weapons. Do you know if they are our friends or are they are just waiting to see which way the wind blows? Providing weapons to our enemies is not a friendly indication that they are on our side.

The World situation should be a wakeup call to the Bush bashers and some conservatives.

If they have a plan to defeat the terrorist, stop Iran and North Korea from building a nuclear arsenal, I have not heard it yet. I have heard a lot of rhetoric about how bad the world situation is, but I have not heard of any solution to solve the problems.

The Fanaticrats want to pull out of Iraq before we win the war. This is absolutely insane. This is telling the terrorist that they have won and the next step is to do whatever they want because they know we have no desire for conflict. This will be an invitation for Iran to take over in Iraq. This will be their first conquest. Next will be Kuwait, Saudi Arabia, and then the Country they hate as bad as the U.S., Israel. Since Russia is a prime provider of War weapons to Iran. The next step is for the two of them to eliminate Great Britain and the U.S.A. Russia already has nuke capabilities and the end of the world is close to completion. North Korea will take over South Korea. Japan will declare war on North Korea because they know they are next on the list. China not to be left out will declare war on Japan. This leaves Iran, Russia and China to fight it out to control the World.

In all reality the United Nations should take action and give Iran and North Korea an ultimatum to halt any plans to develop any atomic weapons. If they fail to comply, the Unite Nation should send in the World Army to take charge until the matter is settled. If the UN would operate as it is supposed to, we would not be under the threat of a North Korea or Iran. I am not in love with the United Nations. I believe we are wasting a lot of money as a member of the UN and are not getting any thing back. Is it time to break away? Iran has thumbed its nose at the USA and the United Nations. It looks like they will not be stopped until military force is brought against them.

I believe the U. S. should have a hit squad of eliminators. Some of these dictators should be stopped before they put millions of there own people in harms way. North Korea is a prime example of a Dictator that spends all his time to evil instead of trying to help his people live a decent civilized life. Look at the difference between North and South Korea. South Korea has a very robust economy, and the people are not starving. They enjoy a very good life style.

CHAPTER 14

CONSTITUTIONAL AMENDMENTS AND ARTICLES TO BE REVISED

AMENDMENT I: AS IT IS CURRENTLY WRITTEN:

Congress shall make no law respecting an establishment of religion, or prohibiting the free exercise thereof; or abridging the freedom of speech, or the press; or the right of the people peaceably to assemble, and petition the Government for a redress of grievances.

AMENDMENT I: PROPOSED AMENDMENT:

Congress shall make no law respecting an establishment of religion, or prohibiting the free exercise thereof; or the right of the people peaceably to assemble, and petition the Government for a redress of grievances; or abridging the freedom of speech, or the press; except in time of war, or conflict with the enemy, that giving solace, comfort, hope, or building the moral of the enemy, is considered treason.

AMENDMENT XIV SECTION 1: AS IT IS CURRENTLY WRITTEN:

All persons born or naturalized in the United States, and subject to the jurisdiction thereof, are citizens of the United States and of the State wherein they reside. No state shall make or enforce any law which shall abridge the privileges or immunities of citizens of the United States; nor shall any State deprive any person of life, liberty, or property, without due process of law, nor deny to any person within its jurisdiction the equal protection of the law.

Proposed Amendment to Amendment XIV Section 1

This proposed amendment was proposed by Representative Ron Paul of Texas jointly with Mr. Alexander 4-28-2005

Section 1 Any person born after the date of the ratification of this article to a mother and father, neither of whom is a citizen of the United States nor a person who owes permanent allegiance to the United States, shall not be a citizen of the United States or of any State solely by reason of birth in the United States.

Section 2 The Congress shall have power to enforce this article by appropriate legislation.

I agree with Mr. Paul and Mr. Alexander, and I encourage all citizens in all the States of the United States to support this amendment.

AMENDMENT XVII: April 8, 1913 AS IT IS CURRENTLY WRITTEN:

The Senate of the United States shall be composed of two Senators from each State, elected by the people thereof, for six years; and each Senator shall have one vote.

The electors in each State shall have the qualifications requisite for electors of the most numerous branch of the State Legislatures. When vacancies happen in the representation of any State in the Senate, the executive authority of such State shall issue writs of election to fill such vacancies: Provided, that the Legislature of any State may empower the Executive thereof to make temporary appointments until the people fill the vacancies by election as the Legislature may direct. This amendment shall not be so construed as to affect the election or term of any Senator chosen before it becomes valid as part of the constitution.

AMENDMENT XVII: April 8, 1913 AS IT SHOULD BE WRITTEN:

The Senate of the United States shall be composed of two Senators from each State, elected by the people thereof, to the office of the Senate no more than twice, for six years; and each Senator shall have one vote. No Person shall be allowed to be elected as Senator of the United States beyond his seventy fourth birthday. The electors in each State shall have the qualifications requisite for electors of the most numerous branch of the state Legislatures.

When vacancies happen in the representation of any State in the Senate, the executive authority of such State shall issue writs of election to fill such vacancies: Provided, That the Legislature of any State may empower the Executive thereof to make temporary appointments until the people fill the vacancies by election as the Legislature may direct. This amendment shall not be so construed as to affect the election or term of any Senator chosen before it becomes valid as part of the Constitution.

ARTICLE. II Section. 2.

The President shall be Commander in Chief of the Army and the Navy of the United States, and of the Militia of the several States, when called into the actual Service of the United States; he may require the opinion, in writing, of the principal Officer in each of the executive Departments, upon any subject relating to the duties of their respective Offices, and he shall have Power to grant Reprieves and Pardons against the United States, except in case of Impeachment.

ARTICLE. II Section. 2. As it should be written

The President shall be Commander in Chief of the Army and the Navy of the United States, and of the Militia of the several States, when called into the actual Service of the United States; he may require the Opinion, in writing , of the Principal Officer in each of the executive Departments, upon any subject relating to the duties of their respective offices, and he shall consult the final decision to grant Reprieves and Pardons against the United States to the full authority of the Supreme Court, except in the Cases of Impeachment, and this matter shall be turned over to the Congress.

ARTICLE. 1. Section. 2 The House of Representatives shall be composed of Members chosen every two Years by the People of the several States, and the Electors in each State shall have the Qualifications requisite for Electors of the most numerous Branch of the State Legislature.

ARTICLE. 1. Section. 2 As it should read. The House of Representatives shall be composed of Members chosen every sixth Year by the People of the several states, and the electors in each State shall have the Qualifications requisite for Electors of the most numerous Branch of the state Legislature. No person shall be elected to the House of Representatives more than twice, for six years, and each Representative shall have one vote. No person shall be allowed to be elected to the office of the House of Representatives beyond their seventy fourth birthday.

AMENDMENTS TO REVISE

I. Congress shall make no law respecting an establishment of religion, or prohibiting the free exercise thereof; or abridging the freedom of speech, or of the press; or the right of the people peaceably to assemble, and to petition the government for a redress of grievances.

XVII; The Senate of the United States shall be composed of two Senators from each State, elected by the people thereof, for six years, and each Senator shall have one vote. The electors in each State shall have the qualifications requisite for electors of the most numerous branch of the State legislatures.

When vacancies happen in the representation of any State in the Senate, the executive authority of such State shall issue writs of elections to fill such vacancies: Provided, That the legislature of any State may empower the executive thereof to make temporary appointments until the people fill the vacancies by election as the legislature may direct.

This amendment shall not be construed as to affect the election or term of any Senator chosen before it becomes valid as part of the Constitution.

XIV; Section 1.

All persons born or naturalized in the United States, and subject to the jurisdiction thereof, are citizens of the United States and of the State wherein they reside. No state shall make or enforce any law which shall abridge the privileges or immunities of citizens of the United States; nor shall any State deprive any person of life, liberty, or property, without due process of law, nor deny to any person within its jurisdiction the equal protection of the law.

XIV. Section 2.

Representatives shall be apportioned among the several States according to their respective numbers, counting the whole number of persons in each State, excluding Indians not taxed. But when the right to vote at any election for the choice of electors for President and Vice President of the United

States, Representatives in Congress, the Executive and Judicial officers of a State, or the members of the Legislature thereof, is denied to any of the male inhabitants of such State, being twenty-one years of age, and citizens of the United States, or in any way abridged, except for participation in rebellion, or other crime, the basis of representation therein shall be reduced in the proportion which the number of such male citizens shall bear to the whole number of male citizens twenty-one years of age in such State.

CHAPTER 15

PATRIOTIC POEMS

RED, WHITE AND BLUE

A Beautiful flag, red, white and blue
With fifty stars, for fifty states, all available for you
It started as a plain piece of cloth
Conceived by the nimble hands of Betsy Ross

A Badge of courage for the World to see
Save the down trodden and set them free
It waves for all who treasure its stand
For freedom and justice throughout the land

A tear in the eye when on a coffin it's draped
A lump in your throat, but it's no mistake
A Hero has sacrificed for what they believe
They would say, "GOD Bless America", but please don't
grieve

The Bugler sounds taps as a last farewell
If this doesn't touch your soul, nothing will
You stand there proud, and thank GOD above
For the U.S.A., the Country we love

Written by:
Harold W. Powell

11/30/04

AMERICA THE GREATEST POEM

We were massed along the Channel on the British side of the shore
We intended to surprise the Germans. Ike had a little surprise for the
Germans in store
It was the largest invasion force that ever was indeed
Our will was strong and minds so brave, we were determined to succeed

The Channel was rough and choppy, our landing craft tried to sink
We tied another alongside; it was dark and black as ink
Every time they splashed together, we jumped to the other side
We knew we could make the jump, if they didn't come untied

The next dawn was a surprise. Our craft was still afloat
We promptly left our host boat, not one of us did choke
We landed short of daybreak, water was about waist deep
It really didn't matter at all, at least we didn't sink

We were one landing craft of thousands in a crowd
The noise from the U S battle ship guns was pleasing but quiet loud
The sands of Normandy was red with GIs blood, you didn't utter a sound
But you dared not reflect on these poor souls,
whose families would be so proud

The Invasion was a spectacle, one never to forget
With thousands of ships of every kind, determined to never quit
Guns a blazing, to drive the enemy out, our troops turned up the heat
It was a job that could not fail, the Germans must face defeat

The Enemy was taken by surprise, thanks to General Ike Dwight
Without his wisdom, and planning, it could have been a loosing fight
I was so proud to be a part, of the largest Invasion of all
I never regretted signing up, even though it was not a ball

When we landed on Normandy Beach
It was a huge step for all mankind
To stop the Devil Hitler, and end War for all time
Many a Hero of America gave their life for the red, white and blue
Don't ever forget their sacrifice, and what they did for you

Our Flag is still flying, a symbol of freedom for all
Keep your finger on the pulse of America, don't let it fall
She is the greatest Nation, don't ever let her down
We must defeat the Terrorist, or they will always be around

10/10/2005
BY: Harold Powell

AMERICAN FREEDOM

America is the greatest
On land, the air and sea
It is the land of freedom
For a life of liberty

Nowhere in this great World
Would I rather be
Than the good ole USA
The stars and stripes for me

For freedom of religion
A right to cherish dear
We have the Constitution
That spells our rights real clear

It's the land of milk and honey
Will it always be this way
You better take an active part
Or your freedom will slip away

CHORUS
Freedom, freedom, is it here to stay
You better wake up America
Or your freedom will slip away

Written by:
Harold Powell
06/27/2005

102

LIBERALS MELODY

Liberals have a tune they always play
Every few Months before Election Day
It's the same old tune, they've used it before
If you vote Republican, Social Security is no more

Medicare is going sky high
Social Security is about to go dry
Gas prices are up because oil is so high
Bush is an oil man and that is why

If Environmentalist had a brain to use
They would immediately stop the production of crude
Force Politicians and Big Oil to comply and sell
Automobiles that run on a Hydrogen Cell

Smoke and smog would soon disappear
Our air and atmosphere would soon be clear
Our lungs would be clean without the smoke
The price of Gasoline is driving me broke

Written By:
Harold Powell
3/26/05

CHAPTER 16

ACKNOWLEDGEMENTS

Bonnie: My very understanding and patient wife. She spent many hours reading and reading again, to correct my mistakes and make suggestions.

Richard Swartz: My very knowledgeable Brother-in-Law, who offered many good suggestions.

Dan Swartz: My Co-Worker, who helped me in my lack of computer knowledge.

Michael Powell: My son who helped me in many computer problems.

Mary Dale: Co-Worker was invaluable for computer answers. I had plenty of questions.

Janie Posey: Friend and valuable assistance in computer help for this publication.

Senator Lugar's Office: For allowing me to use some of his speeches for my book. His Staff in the Indianapolis Office was very kind and helpful to all my requests.

Michelle Proctor: A very dedicated Assistant in Representative Steve Buyers Office in Plainfield, In. who provided me with many Government Articles needed for my book.

The Indianapolis Star: Thanks to the Star for permission to use several articles in their first class newspaper.

The E.P.A. and the U.S. Transportation Department and all the articles on the Internet.

My friend, Greg Black, Attorney: Assistance in changes to the first amendment, and review of the other amendments suggested for proposed changes in this book.

Bruce Bright: For his expertise on computer technology.

Walt O'Riley: Computer expertise.

CHAPTER 17

ABOUT THE AUTHOR

I was born in 1923 and I have seen a lot of changes during that time period to 2007. Growing up in Cloverdale, Indiana, population around 560 people, I spent most of my youth on a rented farm. I was youngest in a family of three brothers and three sisters. My dad was a hard worker, but was not loaded with money. We were lucky enough to rent a house, and with trying to feed a big family, owning a house was almost impossible. We had a big garden which helped feed the family in the summer months and my Mother with the help of the girls, would can enough fruit and vegetables to get us through the winter. We had a cellar which acted as our refrigerant in the summer.

When I was about eight years old, my Dad asked me to go with him to an auction where they were selling a house located at the edge of town. The house was a two story frame with three bedrooms, living room, dining room, kitchen and one indoor bathroom. It had a one car detached garage and work shop. The lot was a nice one acre, mostly fenced. The bidding started low and it was hot and heavy until in got up to five hundred dollars. This looked like this was as high as anyone wanted to go. My Dad asked me what he should do and I said buy it. That was probably the best five hundred he ever spent. After living there for ten years, he had built a small barn and a nice shed. He sold the property for over five thousand dollars. He immediately bought another house he had his eye on. For the rest of his life he never rented again. My Dad buying that first house was my first adventure in Real Estate. I am currently an Agent with RE/MAX Connection in Indianapolis, Indiana. My Owner Broker is a wonderful lady by the name of Shirley Praed.

The first and most valuable help in learning the Realty business was from a very dear friend of my wife and I, Connie Vinton. I was associated with Connie Vinton and John Mills in the Office called Vinton and Mills REALTOR for ten years. I was the first agent to work for Connie who started this firm. I enjoy being a REALTOR and find that it keeps me happy, sometimes wealthy, and always wise.

I attended Cloverdale High School from the first grade through graduation from high school in 1941. While I was in school I mowed yards, and had a paper route delivering The Indianapolis Times. The times was a well known Democrat slanted Newspaper in a Republican town. In a contest I increased the circulation enough to win a weekend trip to Coney Island in Cincinnati, Ohio. Even though my Dad was a staunch Republican, he never mentioned anything about the times. After the paper route and I was old enough to get my drivers license, I upgraded to a position as a runner and all around odd job boy for Denny's Dept. Store in Cloverdale. I counted eggs the farmers brought in to sell so they could buy other food and goods from the store. My other duties consisted of restocking store shelves, delivering groceries to peoples homes, sweep the floors, take out the trash, sometimes if all clerks were busy I would wait on customers.

When Rev. Denny, he also was a Minister, found out I could drive, I even got to be his driver because he never learned to drive. I would take him to the wholesale houses in Indianapolis for supplies and anyplace else he wanted to go.

After graduation from High School, I wanted to make more money, so I got a job with Pickens and Yanders Garage in Cloverdale. I loved cars, so this was a fun job for me. These two great guys taught me a lot about cars. They didn't need any fancy equipment to find what was wrong with the engine. They just cranked it up and listened to it. I have used my experience from this job many times since.

Then along came December 7, 1941, known as Pearl Harbor Day:

I and two friends were hitchhiking to Greencastle, about ten miles North of Cloverdale, to see a movie. Cloverdale did not have a movie theater at the time. Our first ride was going half way which was U.S. 40. At this stop we went into the famous Midway Station Restaurant for a coke. Yes we had cokes back then. It was here that we heard on the radio that Pearl Harbor was being bombed by the Japanese. We had no clue to the location of Pearl Harbor, but we did know a little about Hawaii. We also knew that this was not a good thing. That as you now know was the trigger that ignited the U.S. into WWII.

I was the last of three brothers and a brother-in-law to be drafted into the Military. My Mother, bless her heart, how she must have suffered for over three years with three sons, Hubert, Troy, Myself and her Son in Law, Truman Mannan, all in harms way. I was in the States for four Months training, before we went to Europe. I was in the invasion of France, at Omaha Beach in Normandy on June 6, 1944. I tell everybody that I spent my first night in France at the Fox Hole Motel. My brother Hubert was in the Air Force, brother Troy was in the Coast Guard, brother in law Truman was in the Infantry. He received the Bronze Star for clearing land mines out of the way with a bayonet so his outfit could advance on the enemy.

After being over in Europe for about two years and eight Months I was back in the good old U.S.A.

I was discharged and arrived back home on January 4, 1946 which was my Mothers Birthday. She said that it was the best Birthday she ever had.

What you just read was mostly about me. Now what I want you to read is mostly about you and what you and I are going to do. We are going to save this great Nation. I am going to be very specific about what needs to be done to make our original founders of this the greatest Country in the world proud of us.

I do know one thing for certain. You, yes you, that means you. You never vote, you never contact your Senators or Representatives. You keep complaining, but not to the right people. Well, Mr. and Mrs. America, keep it up and Washington will assume that they are doing a great job because they haven't heard any complaints. Do you enjoy your freedom? Do you know how many wars have been fought and how many great Americans have died to protect your freedom? Now get you head on straight and get out there and vote. Pay attention to what is going on. It is crucial to start now. One person can make a difference and Bill O'Reilly of Fox News has proven this.

APPENDIX

FOR IMMEDIATE RELEASE

Date: 7/12/06

TWA Flight 800 Federal Law Suit for 'missing evidence' Filed Today

Flight 800 Independent Researchers Organization (FIRO) is filing a federal complaint against the National Transportation Safety Board (NTSB) for data and information related to the crash of TWA Flight 800. Specifically, FIRO is suing for documents regarding the chain of custody of evidence.

One wreckage item in particular was described as possibly being the "smoking gun" by FIRO Chairman Dr. Tom Stalcup. The wreckage exited Flight 800's airframe at apparent supersonic speeds and landed about a half mile closer to JFK airport than any other piece of wreckage. The Navy recovered it, but it never made it to the reconstruction hangar.

Flight 800 exploded and crashed south of Long Island, NY on July 17, 1996. Witnesses saw a streak of light rise from the ocean surface before the crash, indicating a missile attack. Ultimately federal investigators dismissed the missile theory due to an apparent lack of physical evidence. And the NTSB announced the an electrical short-circuit most likely caused one of the jetliner's fuel tanks to explode, although no conclusive evidence for this short-circuit was discovered.

FIRO researchers determined that Navy divers recovered the high-speed wreckage. It's listed "recovered (confirmed)" on a Navy salvage map, but is not listed in the NTSB's official debris field data base. Other wreckage disappeared from the reconstruction hangar according to investigators, and FIRO's law suit seeks information on this other wreckage as well.

Radar sites recorded the wreckage flying off the aircraft's right side, on a southerly course, which matches eyewitness accounts. The witnesses saw an object head southbound and then explode when it reached Flight 800. This object's momentum, together with the force of its explosion can explain the radar data and the Navy's recovery location of the high-speed wreckage.

For more information, as well as an instructional video on the radar data and this wreckage, see http://Flight800.org

Contact: Tom Stalcup, FIRO Chairman, 774-392-0856

Key evidence, confirmed recovered, now missing, Flight 800

July 14, 2004

Documents recently obtained under ongoing FOIA litigation describe how the FBI had a policy of withholding "suspicious" physical evidence from the National Transportation Safety Board (NTSB). And today, a key piece of evidence recovered by the Navy is still missing.

The NTSB said a spark in a fuel tank caused the crash, and that they had "no physical evidence" of a missile engagement. But did the FBI's evidence-withholding policy effectively keep physical evidence from the NTSB?

Perhaps, but what is certain is that the very first piece of wreckage that left the plane (FAA radar recorded it flying off the plane at apparent supersonic speeds[1] just as Flight 800 explodes) is now missing. It's listed "confirmed recovered" on Navy charts, but is nowhere to be found on the NTSB's.

This piece of wreckage may very well be the key to the crash. But its trajectory, speed, and recovery location all contradict the official theory. It was blown out perpendicular to the flight path and landed more than 1/4 mile too close to

JFK airport to fit within the official "spark" scenario. Rather than explaining what accelerated it, why it landed so close to JFK, or how it vanished from the reconstruction hangar, the Safety Board remained, and continues to remain conspicuously silent.

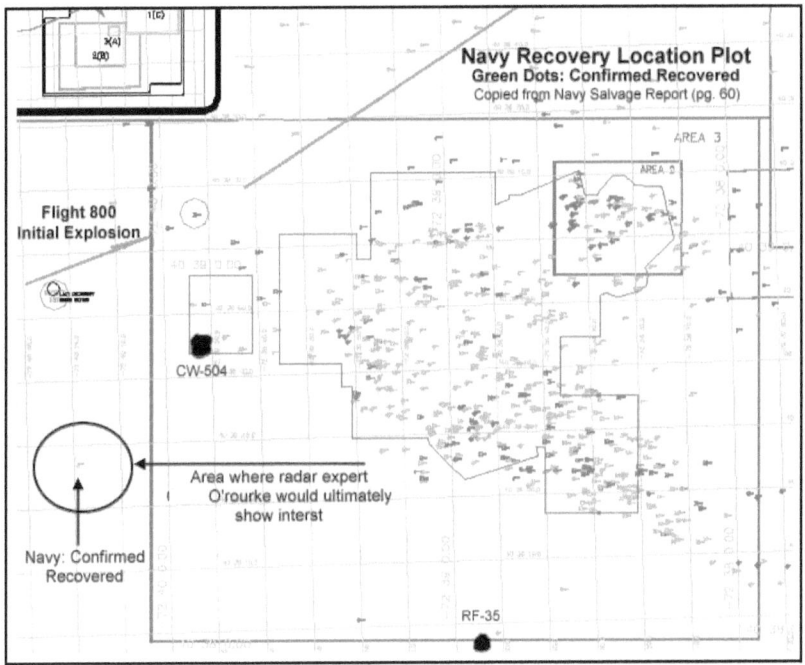

A little history

Prior to 9/11, TWA Flight 800 was perhaps the most watched airliner disaster in history. More than 700 witnesses provided the FBI with their accounts.[1]

Many said an object rose off the ocean surface and collided with Flight 800. But without corroborating physical evidence, the Feds didn't believe them. Some investigators, however, thought they had supporting evidence. But they complained that it disappeared into the FBI's "black hole" of a crime lab in Washington, according to a New York Times article published a month after the crash.[2]

The final word, as far as the government was concerned, came in August 2000 during a so-called "sunshine hearing." The NTSB said a spark in a fuel tank caused the crash. Case closed. But for those following the case, the hearing was far from illuminating.

Absent from the hearing was any explanation of the crucial, high-speed wreckage described above. Usually quite valuable to investigators, wreckage that separates early during a plane crash sometimes holds the key to solving the accident. But this time, the NTSB seemed disinterested. They didn't even seem concerned that it disappeared.

A little mystery

Some time after Navy divers recovered it from the ocean floor, the wreckage vanished. It's listed in the Navy's salvage map, but not in the NTSB's. And just as inexplicable as its disappearance, the NTSB turned a blind eye to its radar-recorded trajectory.[3] Fortunately however, not everyone was towing the NTSB line.

A radar consultant hired by the FBI during the investigation concluded that "some portion or component of the aircraft kicked out to the right nearly immediately after the loss of the transponder signal." When he couldn't locate any such wreckage pattern in official debris field maps, the consultant wrote, "I became quite curious as to what portions of the aircraft these could be."[4]

But the NTSB was apparently less curious. They never mentioned the wreckage at the sunshine hearing, didn't show it on their debris field map, and didn't make a single reference to it in their final report. Some concerned experts sent in a petition, requesting an explanation for this fast, radar-tracked wreckage. The NTSB wrote back about a year later saying they covered it in the final report.[5]

They didn't. The final report devotes more space to false radar returns and nearby ships than to the abundant and telling radar returns from the aircraft itself. Nothing on the wreckage described above.[6]

So where did the wreckage go, and why was it ignored?

Mystery explained?

Documents obtained recently during ongoing FOIA litigation describe how the FBI screened all recovered wreckage before handing it over to the NTSB. According to one such document, the FBI withheld over 300 suspicious wreckage items from the NTSB for "further investigation."[7] The earliest wreckage may have been withheld in this manner and sent to the FBI lab in Washington--the one investigators described as a "black hole"[2].

Perhaps the corresponding radar evidence was ignored simply because it conflicted with the NTSB's spark scenario. Like the tell-tale explosion signature recorded by a black box, explosive residues in the cargo compartment, witnesses who swear they saw a missile, and other evidence, the NTSB repeatedly dismissed evidence that didn't fit within their theory.

The NTSB's Metallurgy/Structures Sequencing Group all but admitted this practice in their factual report, which explained how they "strove to fit a proposed scenario to all relevant observations ... [and] had to accept that some feature(s) either could not be explained by the proposed scenario or might even be in conflict with the proposed scenario."[8]

This meant that at least one NTSB group "strove" to fit the spark theory to their observations, while feeling they "had to" accept that some feature(s) may conflict with this theory. I wonder if the NTSB Radar Group felt the same way when they noticed wreckage flying out the right side of the aircraft at apparent super-sonic speeds[1].

Until the Feds open up and truly shed light onto the key pieces of evidence, the public can only guess what happened to Flight 800. But for many of the witnesses, what happened is no mystery. The neglected evidence doesn't conflict with their observations. Rather, it corroborates their accounts of a missile engagement.[2]

References

[1] NTSB Exhibit 4A, Witness Group Factual Report, available at www.ntsb.gov

[2] THE NEW YORK TIMES: Behind a Calm Facade Investigation Embodied Chaos, Distrust, Stress. Joe Sexton, 08/23/96.

[3] NTSB Exhibit 13A, available at www.ntsb.gov

[4] FBI Report by Radar Consultant Michael O'Rourke, FIRO Petition, Attachment II, available at http://Flight800.org/FIRO_pet_attach.pdf

[5] FIRO Petition and NTSB Response to Petition, available at http://Flight800.org/probable_cause.htm

[6] NTSB Final Report on Flight 800, available at www.ntsb.gov

[7] FBI Report on Bomb Tech Activities, recently obtained during ongoing FOIA litigation (Sephton vs. FBI, 01-2502). Available upon request.

[1]FAA radar recorded this wreckage traveling at an average speed of

approximately 500 mph over four seconds. Because wreckage exiting an aircraft rapidly decreases its speed due to the extreme force of air resistance, this piece of wreckage most likely had an initial velocity far greater than the speed of sound, which, at Flight 800's altitude was approximately 700 mph.

[2]Witnesses on Long Island reported seeing a fast moving, flare-like object in near-level flight approach Flight 800 from the aircraft's left (north-facing) side. Such an intercept is consistent with wreckage immediately exiting Flight 800's right side, and not the left, as radar data indicates. Witness 649 (name redacted and numbered by the NTSB) is a good example of such a witness. Read his account at the NTSB's website, here: Exhibit 4A, Appendix H.